To: Joyo

We are so
that you can
worship with us

Happy Mother's ♡ ♡

May God bless
you as you
read +

Live
Lighter!

40 Days
Lighter

-♡-

Andrea
Stli

40 Days

Lighter

A DEVOTIONAL JOURNEY FOR WOMEN
DETERMINED TO LIVE FREE

ANDREA T. ST. LOUIS

Foreword by Hewlette Pearson

XULON PRESS

Xulon Press
2301 Lucien Way #415
Maitland, FL 32751
407.339.4217
www.xulonpress.com

Printed in the United States of America.

ISBN-13: 9781545621363

DEDICATION

To my men –

my darling husband, Matthew,

& our incredible sons, Ethan & Isaac

Thank you for loving this woman
on her journey to freedom!

TABLE OF CONTENTS

ACKNOWLEDGMENTS

I would like to say Thank You, first and foremost, to God for the transformative journey I am on, and the grace to share this journey with others.

Special Thank You to Katishia Gallishaw for your incredible support throughout this project. Thank you for acting on what God allowed you to see in me, for pushing me to write, and holding me accountable to finish what I started. May God return to you, multiplied exponentially, all that you have invested in me on this journey.

Thank you to Dr. Tonya Williams for calling forth the author in me; to Pastor Hewlette Pearson for watering that word in me, and for your willingness to be a part of this journey. You have truly been a mentor and guide as I have walked this path. Thank you both for allowing the Lord to use you to give meaning to my future.

To my husband Matthew, our beautiful boys, Ethan & Isaac – there aren't enough words to explain how much I love you. To my family, the Flynn's, Gedeon's, St. Louis's, Carter's, and Daubon's–I know I'm a handful. Thank you for believing in my dreams.

To my sisters who walked with me on my life's "40 days lighter journey," and who continue to journey with me on this path to freedom. Whitney Wilfred and Ashley Ramsey, thank you for loving me through the tough stuff and celebrating the woman who continues to emerge.

To Reginald (Reggie) Jennings and Keshia Maxwell – I can never repay you both for taking my health as seriously as your own. You taught me to find joy in the discipline of caring for this body – and leg day is everything!

Thank you to all those who supported me on this journey, and invested their finances, prayers, platform, or expertise in me to bring this book to life: Matthew St. Louis, Doyle & Evangeline St. Louis, Hannah St. Louis, Robert & Rebekah Carter, Sydonia (Barry) & Camille Blake, Carleen Charles, Paulette Barrett, Vonetta Walker, Nicole Griffin, Crystal Senter-Brown, Revival Time Evangelistic Center, and many other friends and family members both near and far. I appreciate you all.

And last, but certainly not least – Thank you to my readers, for making the choice to join me on this journey to a life lived lighter.

FOREWORD

*I*f we had the power to add more minutes or hours to time, we would, if only to get more things done. But I believe we have been given something greater— the power to make the most of the time given. Carpe diem! Seize the day! The ability to do what we can with the time we have is a gracious gift from God. And part of "doing what we can" also involves taking care of self. 40 Days Lighter is an oasis in the busyness of life. It's a fresh approach to finding the path to rest, rejuvenation, healing, and you...again.

Because I was intentional about reading the manuscript for the writing of this foreword, I decided to set aside time to literally walk myself through this devotional. As I neared the end of the first instruction given at the beginning of part one, I found myself becoming more relaxed than normal. The closing of my eyes, a calculated slowness in exhaling my breath, and an intentional resting of my shoulders and arms brought a moment of peace and rest...And then a sudden jarring as I wrestled with the momentum of gravity to prevent my tablet from falling from my hands to the floor.

Could the rest of the devotional lead me into a deeper actualization of the need to just let things go and be overwhelmed by the moment of "now"—the opportunity to stop the busyness of life and just be? Well, I read on...

At times, I felt as if I were a bystander witnessing some of the true-to-life stories Andrea shared along the journey, and at other times I wanted to say, "Stay out of my business, woman!" The truths and principles found in this devotional are impactful. The practical steps and exercises will challenge you in your thinking and perception of self, while helping to lead you into the awe-inspiring way our Creator sees us. You will find that He is intentional about getting us in position to living our life dreams "lighter."

If you follow the directives offered through Andrea's pen, you are sure to experience change on multiple levels! I summarize the change as a healing that takes place to bring wholeness to our physical, emotional, mental and spiritual being, and financial state. Maulana Jalaluddin Rumi, a 13th century Persian poet said, "The wound is the place where The Light enters you." The life experiences that have left us wounded and broken are perfect for God's Light to enter and to heal. No longer do we need to continue living life with some semblance of normalcy while lacking true wholeness and joy. The time has come for us to turn to and run to the Light of God's presence. In so doing, we will be overwhelmed by the healing we desperately need.

I believe this devotional is in your hands right now because you need this time...you and God...alone. You're now ready for an intimate journey together. Carpe diem! Where will you go? Up. How will you feel? Lighter!

Hewlette Pearson
Author, Motivator, Educator & Pastor

Part I

BREATHING ROOM

"As the deer pants for streams of water,
so my soul pants for you, my God.
My soul thirsts for God, for the living God."
Psalm 42:1-2 (NIV)

*D*o this exercise with me, just for a moment. Close your eyes. Inhale deeply and then slowly exhale. Be still for just a moment or two afterwards.

If you need an image on which to focus, choose one of the descriptions below. Now close your eyes and imagine them. Experience them. Feel them.

- That first free breath through BOTH nostrils right after the congestion from a head cold dissipates.

- Being boxed in by buzzing, chit-chatting, humming passengers on a crowded elevator going down 10 floors, finally reaching your floor and stepping off. *Ah, into open silence.*

Alright, finished imagining?

First, pat yourself on the back because I'm pretty sure you took a moment out of your busy day to just breathe as you envisioned each scene.

Second – did you feel that?!

In case you are unsure what you should have felt, it was the liberating experience of allowing the air to fill your lungs, and then exhaling to release it to the atmosphere. Hopefully, in this small moment you might have taken from the busyness of your jam-packed schedule, you also released a bit of the tension. Yes, that tension sitting right at the base of your neck, or buried deep within the fibers of your shoulder muscle.

In the same way that pausing to breathe deeply and letting go of the stiff positioning of our muscles brings more freedom, flexibility in movement, and even greater range of motion in our bodies, letting go of the "clutter" in our minds, hearts and lives releases us to embrace our purpose.

Clearing out the clutter, turning down the noise, tuning out the distractions, simplifying our schedules, releasing the mental, emotional, and spiritual burdens that weigh us down, all help to free us to think, be, do, and breathe.

If you are reading this and saying – "I need to feel that feeling, I need to breathe" – pause with me, just for a moment, and pray this prayer:

"God, I empty my heart before you. I let these tears fall as a sign of release, of surrender. I'm desperate for more of Your Spirit, more of Your Presence, but right now, I have so much clutter, mentally, emotionally, spiritually, and physically, that sometimes it can be hard to recognize Your gentle tug on my heartstrings. The unnecessary distractions have made it hard to experience true freedom in Your Presence, becoming instead a prison from which I yearn to escape. Today, I declare liberty, I speak life, I release my cares, casting my burdens on You because You care for me. Be my guide through this 40 days, and like Christ, let me emerge ready to fulfill my assignment."

Now go ahead, and BREATHE.

Day 1 – Coming Up for Air

When I was 5 years old, I had a near-drowning experience.

A relative had taken my sister, cousin and me to the park to enjoy the sunshine, and though I don't remember much of the moments leading up to the incident, that day is forever emblazoned into my long-term memory.

I vividly recall watching and feeding the ducks floating in the park pond, and though the sun was beaming down, there was still a slight breeze in the air. I've always been small for my age (in terms of stature), so to maximize my reach, I was standing at the very edge of the walkway to make sure that the ducks got the bread.

Twenty-five years later, and I still have no clue what caused my child size feet to leave the walkway, as I slipped straight into the pond. Yet I will never forget my summer dress and spring jacket-wearing frame landing fully in the water and beginning to sink.

For years to come, I would be traumatized by the deafening silence, and limbo-like weightlessness, I experienced in those moments that seemed to last an eternity. Thrashing and panicking, I tried with all my little might to find something, *anything* to hold on to and pull myself up. I can still see the bright sun glittering through the water above me, as my mouth and nose filled with liquid, and my 5-year-old heart filled with fear.

I just wanted a breath. One, solitary, water-free breath.

In my, uninformed, inexperienced, non-swimming mind, I thought if I could just inhale some air, from *somewhere*, I would be okay. Of course, the only thing I pulled in was… more water. I did, however, know enough to recognize that the growing discomfort in my chest might mean I was drowning.

(To be continued…)

Some of us have lived, day in and day out, with the unnerving sense that we are going under. We are drowning in the depths of unfulfilled expectations, unrequited love, abandoned hopes, and deferred dreams. We are drowning in a sea of debt, an ocean of "urgent" work, or maybe in the lake of unaddressed emotional turmoil. We are drowning and desperate for deliverance. And like most desperate people, *we will do just about anything* to find a solid place to stand or something firm to hold onto.

Yet just about everything we've tried has failed. Every person we thought could save us has fallen short of their superhero designation. Being in a relationship didn't help us. Getting married didn't stop the drowning feeling. That new job certainly didn't put an end to the growing sense of despair. Even shopping wasn't quite the therapy we thought it would be. *As a matter of fact, no external changes have done anything about this internal struggle to* come up for air.

The truth is, we cannot save ourselves. We do have a part to play in our deliverance process, (which we'll discuss later), but the reality is that we are all in need of a Savior. And it isn't a bird, it isn't a plane, it certainly isn't a rich man using his family's fortune to dress in a black bat suit. The only Savior we have, the only Lifeguard qualified to pull us up from the depths is Jesus Christ.

Today, hear His voice beckoning us:

"Come to me, all you who are weary and
burdened, and I will give you rest."
Matthew 11:28 (NIV)

And like the psalmist David, let our hearts cry out in response:

"Hear my cry, O God; listen to my prayer.
From the ends of the earth I call to you, I call as my
heart grows faint; lead me to the
rock that is higher than I."
Psalm 61:1-2 (NIV)

Reflect:

1. What is making you feel overwhelmed, and how long have you felt that way? Why?

2. Where have you turned for help? Have you reached out to family, friends, mentors or spiritual leader? Have they been able to help? Why or why not?

3. When is the last time you brought your burdens to the Lord in prayer? Do you leave them there, or do you carry them with you when you get up from your knees?

Day 2 – In the Stillness

*"For years to come, I would be traumatized by the deafening silence, and limbo-like weightlessness, I experienced in those moments that seemed like an eternity. Thrashing and panicking, I tried with all my little might to find something, **anything**, to hold on to and pull myself up. I can recall the bright sun glittering through the water above me, as my mouth and nose filled with liquid, and my 5-year-old heart **filled with fear**."*

What I found most unnerving in those moments under the water, was the extreme quiet and stillness beneath the pond's surface. Robbed of sound, but not sight, seemingly of gravity, but not weightless enough to float to the top, my anxiety began to shoot through the roof.

This memory became so embedded in my brain, that, when triggered in my psyche, I would have vivid flashbacks, even into late adolescence, complete with sights, smells, and the distinct lack of sound. My mother will verify that washing my hair became an arduous and most undesirable task, as she endured loud, tearful accusations that she was trying to drown me, should the water from the faucet come streaming into my ears or face.

I simply could not stand the thought of being without the senses that helped to orient me in the world. Sight and sound, working together, helped me to find my direction and maintain my equilibrium and balance. The interrupted awareness was more than I could bear.

There have been seasons in life where I have felt stripped of my awareness of God's Presence. Moments when I felt like I couldn't hear him or find anything to hold on to. Many of us have experienced times in life where we might be surrounded by people—family, friends, or coworkers, just as I was surrounded by water—yet we feel so alone, and unable to connect.

We feel as though we are in a perpetual state of limbo, not sure which way is up, unsure of the way forward. We are longing for someone to come and take us by the hand, to pull us up out of the deep waters of despair. *Unable to see our help, our coming deliverance from our submerged position, we begin to fear the worst.*

The truth is, we can never sink so deep into the waters of trouble that God's Presence cannot reach us.

The psalmist David declares,

"Where can I go from Your spirit? Where can I flee from Your Presence? If I go up to the heavens, you are there; if I make my bed in the depths, you are there."
Psalm 139:7-8 (NIV)

He recognizes that there is nowhere so deep, dark or distant that God's eyes cannot see him. And he doesn't just say that God is sitting up in the cosmos somewhere, looking down from the throne. No! He says, wherever I could fathom to be, You (GOD) are there!

No matter how still, how silent, how isolating your situation may feel right now, know that God is with you. His Word yet speaks to you and to me.

Like the prophet, Elijah, in 1 Kings 19, we may feel like we are tired of the fight, depressed and ready to give up. And as we listen for the voice of the Lord, we hear the wind, but the Lord is not in the wind. There is an earthquake, but the Lord is not in the earthquake; a fire but the Lord is not in the fire.

Oh, but the stillness. The nerve-wracking, sensory-depriving, distraction-eliminating silence is the place where we can hear the still small Voice of the Lord Almighty.

Don't despise the stillness, despite its discomfort. Maybe the Lord is just trying to get your attention.

Reflect:

1. When is the last time you felt like you couldn't feel God's Presence? Describe that feeling.

2. How do you find assurance that God is with you even He seems silent?

3. In your silent season, have you looked to other voices for answers? Was the response helpful or harmful in the long run?

Day 3 – Love Lifted Me

"He reached down from on high and took hold of me;
he drew me out of deep waters."
Psalm 18:16 (NIV)

Now, to be fair, it was in no way my uncle's fault that I fell into the pond.

My little sister and cousin, energetic and excited as they were, had run on ahead to another area of the park, long bored with the serene ducks. Naturally, my uncle went after them, assuming that I was following right behind him. And I should have been but lingered a moment longer for one last look.

Isn't that just how some of us treat sin? Idling behind for one last look, touch, or taste, when God is calling us to come on and move forward. But that's a lesson for another day.

My poor uncle's heart must have missed a beat when he realized that the one kid that everyone can count on to be where she's supposed to be, was nowhere to be found.

What alerted him to my predicament in the pond, I will never know. Yet I am positive that I will never forget the sight of his hand reaching down for me, grabbing hold of my jacket and lifting me upwards and into his arms. Relief is far too mild a word to describe what I felt in that moment.

I was five when I learned what it meant for someone to *save my life.* Five.

Every time I think of God "saving" someone, I see that image of the strong hand reaching down to me through the glistening water. In His love, God pulls us up out of the muck and mire of our lives, regardless of how we ended up in the mess in the first place!

What does it mean to be lifted by the love of God?

One – You are seen! When life gets overwhelming, it is easy to believe that we are walking around in an invisibility cloak, and the proverbial "no one" can *see* what we are going through. "No one understands my pain. No one knows or cares how I'm hurting." We get so inwardly focused, that we altogether forget there is a God who sees when we are missing in action.

Two – You are worth the reach! My uncle must have known that his shirt or whatever he was wearing would get wet, but he reached in and pulled me up anyway. John 3:16 is a perfect illustration of God's view that we are worth the reach.

"For God so loved the world that he gave his one and only Son, that whoever believes in him shall not perish but have eternal life."
John 3:16 (NIV)

The truth is that loving us cost God Someone precious— His Only Son. Yet He chose to love us anyway!

Three – We are now safe in our Creator's arms. If I never appreciated a hug from my uncle before, I was more than grateful for his warm embrace after experiencing the fright of my life, still shaken, dripping wet, and cold. I was no longer under water, scared and struggling. Instead, being in his arms brought to me the awareness that I had been rescued. In the same way, knowing that my life rests safely in God's hands, I can truly say that I have been rescued!

Reflect:

1. Have you let God's rescuing, lifting love fill your heart today? If you have not experienced that love, but desire to, pray this simple prayer with me:

   Dear God, I desire to know your love that saves, rescues and delivers. I have been drowning in my own doubts, fears, and inability to change myself, but I am now aware that You are the Lifeguard who is mighty to save. Please, let your lifting love fill my life today. Amen.

2. Think of a time when the love of God came and lifted you out of a desperate place or situation. Be creative – draw what that moment felt like, and how it continues to impact you. Or if you prayed the prayer above, draw what you are feeling right now!

Day 4 – Breathe In, Breathe Out

"I will exalt you, Lord, for you lifted me out of the depths and did not let my enemies gloat over me. Lord my God, I called to you for help, and you healed me."
Psalm 30:1-2 (NIV)

Free from the clutches of my watery prison, I began to cough and sputter, expelling the water in my mouth and nose. More importantly, I was breathing air, free and clear; but the sheer terror of what I had experienced, caused me to cry and hyperventilate and *forget to breathe.*

"You're okay. Just breathe," are the words I vaguely recall spoken to me in the moments following my rescue.

I was no longer floundering in the water, but my mind and heart needed time to catch up to my body. Traumatic experiences can have this effect on many of us. Even though the alarming or tragic event has passed, our minds and emotions struggle to get in sync with this news.

Yet, if we are to ever experience the fullness of real "breathing room," at some point, we must transition from living in the place of pain, and begin to move towards healing.

My falling in that pond at the age of five, would have long-lasting impact on my psyche, even though the emergency had passed. The fear that filled my heart in those moments beneath the water, remained with me as I grew, preventing me from learning to swim for another 13 years, causing anxiety every time I drove over a bridge, and even determining which seat I would be in when I flew (no windows please)!

My inability to move beyond the trauma of that moment inevitably forced me to relive the horror of sinking in the water every time my hair was washed; even a fun day at the beach would go south as water splashed in my face.

Now that I'm able to breathe freely and experience ease in the presence of large bodies of water, I think of all the memory-making moments I have missed, out of fear. I realized that it was not until I could tell myself, "You're okay Andrea. Just breathe," that I was able to see the present moment as separate and distinct from that fateful day at the park.

I am by no means saying that you will ever forget the pain or hurt or trauma of the difficult moment you may have faced. I certainly have not, or you would not be reading my story in these pages. What I can say, is that when we give ourselves permission to get into God's Presence, a wondrous exchange takes place.

Just as the body needs to breathe in oxygen to bring new life to our cells, and breathe out the carbon dioxide that has built up and needs to be expelled, our spirit needs this same refreshing and renewal. **As we breathe in His grace, His peace, His restoring love, we can then**

**breathe out the fear, anxiety, and perpetual agony
of life's difficult moments.**

We invite God's healing flow to make us new, to the point
that He can use what we've been through to reach and
rescue someone else.

Reflect:

1. Have you invited God's healing flow to redeem
   your hurt and move you from your place of pain
   into a place of purpose?

2. Your testimony of God's love has tremendous
   power to extend a lifeline to someone else. Write
   it down and share it with someone today.

3. Breathing Exercise & Prayer:

- Go to a quiet spot, maybe with some soft worship
  music playing in the background.

- Slowly breathe in for 10 seconds (or for as long
  as you can). As you breathe, silently thank God
  for His grace, peace, and healing filling you and
  flowing to you in this moment.

- Now slowly release the breath, again silently,
  thanking God for taking the fear, worry, doubt,
  and hurt that has kept you from living free.

Day 5 – Breathe into Me

"Then the Lord God formed a man from the dust of the
ground and breathed into his nostrils the breath of life,
and the man became a living being."
Genesis 2:7 (NIV)

One of the primary signs of life is breath. The inflating
and deflating of our lungs, the expanding and con-
tracting of our diaphragm, and the sensation of air
passing through our nostrils or mouth are all clear indi-
cations that we are still alive.

When such signs are absent, life-saving measures
must be employed. A common emergency procedure
performed when someone is not breathing is Cardio
Pulmonary Resuscitation, or CPR. During CPR, the intention is to get oxygen to the afflicted person's vital organs,
especially the brain, by ensuring that the lungs continue
to take in air, and the heart continues to pump the oxy-
genated blood.

Thankfully, my harrowing, near-drowning experience
did not require any further life-sustaining measures
once I was pulled up from the water.

Yet I have experienced heartaches in my life that have
left me feeling as though I needed spiritual or emotional
resuscitation.

In addition to the absence of breathing activity, someone
in need of CPR may have lips that have turned blue,

growing cold. They are unresponsive, no matter how vigorously you attempt to rouse them. Their pulse may be fading, faint, or absent, and other signs of life may be disappearing.

There have been times when I have felt like an inanimate lump of clay, incapable of life or movement, unable to live or love, in danger of drying out, turning to stone, and returning to the dust from which I was created. My pulse and passion for life grew faint, nearly undetectable, and I began to lose my ability to *feel*. My compassion, empathy, and general care for others, all but disappeared. My speech was no longer warmed with love and grace, but had gone cold with bitterness and resentment.

I needed someone to breathe into me and restore the signs of life. I needed the flow of spiritual sustenance to be re-established, enabling the parts of me that relied on this "life force" – my spirit and soul – to survive.

I needed God to breathe into me, and cause me to live!

The beauty of God's life-giving breath, is that unlike with physical CPR, He never expects us to breathe on our own. We can rely on His Spirit to revive us, moment by moment, and day by day, no matter the ways that life or the enemy attempts to leave us breathless.

If you are in a place where you feel like you can't breathe, as though you've gotten the wind knocked out of you, and you are unable to catch your breath, you may need resuscitation. Your prayer life has all but ceased, your passion has disappeared, your relationships are all on life support, and you simply can't find any strength to move forward.

I am here to let you know that there is a Healer, a Restorer, One who revives us with His life-giving breath, imparting His very Spirit to us.

Reflect:

1. Today, if you are feeling lifeless and out of breath, *ask God to breathe into you again.*

2. Write down the areas of your life that feel lifeless, and pray over them. Be specific about what caused this condition, or ask for clarity to identify the root cause.

3. Once you have identified the lifeless areas, check out these passages of Scripture: Genesis 2:7, Ezekiel 37:1-10, Psalm 104:27-30, Acts 17:24-28. As you meditate on these verses that show God as Life-giver, write your thoughts about them below. Commit to releasing every are of your life into His hands.

Part II

RELEASE

$\mathcal{W}$e all have moments when people, emotions, resources, and opportunities come into our lives, to serve a purpose, for a time, and at the end of that time must be released.

There are seasonal friendships, temporary relationships, and if we're honest, passing infatuations. We experience a full gamut of ever-fluctuating emotions that help us to cope, process, and ultimately face life's difficult circumstances. We grow into and out of clothing – whether vertically or horizontally – as we age, and our bodies transform. Doors of opportunity open and close with the regularity of a healthy heartbeat. We daily experience the reality of money passing through our hands and bank accounts, coming in and going out in exchange for goods and services. Even the food that enters our body must find a path to release – some parts to be expended as energy and others to be expelled as waste.

In each of these cases, something has come to us – into our minds, hearts, bodies or lives – yet ultimately has a time to make its exit. Trouble happens when the time for release arrives and we find ourselves unwilling or unable to let go of what we have received. There are physical and mental illnesses caused by the body's inability to release a chemical, byproduct or toxin. Debilitating emotional afflictions can be triggered when our conscious or subconscious mind remains imprisoned by the trauma and hurt we have experienced, making us unable to break free of the grip of that moment. Death occurs if the lungs do not take in oxygen and release carbon monoxide.

Individuals who find it difficult or outright impossible to let go of the items that have come into their lives are known as *hoarders*. They are often ostracized and isolated, and become withdrawn when their overwhelmingly cluttered lifestyle is discovered. A hoarder's inability to separate from "stuff" often leaves little room for the people who matter most, and creates a cumbersome lifestyle, navigated through limited, confining and often hazardous or unsafe quarters.

Spiritual, mental and emotional hoarding can have the same effect on our lives, limiting our potential and our ability to move forward. It can stifle our vision for the future and suppress our gifts meant to be used to the benefit of others.

Life is meant to be lived in a cycle of *receiving* and *releasing*, and without this order, life comes to a halt altogether. Over the next five days, it is my prayer that you will be encouraged to find the will to release – letting go of negative thoughts and emotions, like doubt, fear, or bitterness – and liberating yourself to share the best of who you are with the world.

Day 6 – Possessed by Our Possessions

"Jesus answered, "If you want to be perfect, go, sell
your possessions and give to the poor, and you will
have treasure in heaven. Then come, follow me."
When the young man heard this, he went away sad,
because he had great wealth."
Matthew 19:21-22 (NIV)

In Matthew 19, we are introduced to a wealthy young
man, someone accustomed to having plenty, and likely
not acquainted with much want. In Matthew 19:16,
we find him asking Jesus what he needed to do to gain
something else—in this case, eternal life. Jesus tells him
to keep the commandments, naming them at the young
man's request. Yet somehow, despite acknowledging
that he has kept the commandments, he asks the Great
Teacher the most important question of his life: *"What
do I still lack?"*

This man, who was likely unfamiliar with the idea of
'doing without,' was aware that in spite of his best efforts,
something was still missing in his life. Unfortunately, we
get a front row seat to a true tragedy—far more commonplace than we want to admit—when Jesus gives the
man clear instructions to sell what he owns, give to the
poor, and follow Him. Verse 22 tells us that the young
man, hearing Jesus's words, "went away sad, because he
had great wealth" (Matthew 19:22, NIV).

He recognized that there was something greater than his
possessions to be gained – eternal life. He acknowledged

that despite following the commandments, he was still missing something important. *Yet when offered the process by which to obtain what he desired, he could not bear the thought of losing the wealth he already possessed, even though the value of eternal life outweighed it all.*

We all reach points in our lives where we must make a choice: to hold on to who we have been or what we have done, or to change and do something different; to keep a tight grip on the money we have, or invest it in making a better life, for ourselves and for others. We must choose how we use our time, talents, and treasure. We decide what and how much we give of ourselves to others, or opt to seclude ourselves and our fortunes to lonely castles that fade and crumble with time.

This young man found himself possessed by his possessions, and owned by what he owned, instead of being the master he might have thought himself to be. To this man, his possessions and status were everything – though in the grand scheme of life, they were but a small sacrifice to make for something greater. He couldn't not see or understand the eternal rate of return for such a seemingly significant investment.

In the absence of the balance of giving and receiving, obtaining and releasing, the flow in and the flow out – of money, people, resources, and even the air we breathe – we find ourselves woefully weighed down, heavy, unable to move forward, and ultimately suffocating to death.

Moments of release open us up to new, greater possibilities for the days, months and years ahead. Only when a crop has been harvested, and the land has been cleared, can the ground be properly prepared to embrace a new growing season. God hasn't made you a reservoir, but a channel of His grace, goodness and love, to reach the people around you.

Failure to release what we have been given to others, simultaneously closes us off from the possibility of receiving as well. If we tighten our hands into a fist, to maintain a tight grip on what we already possess, we strip ourselves of the ability to receive anything further into our hands. Rather than preserving our hold on our possessions, our belongings begin to have a hold on us.

We must learn to live life with our hearts and hands wide open, so that we can both give and receive, always with the possibility of obtaining something greater.

Reflect:

1. What resource, gift, talent or opportunity are you afraid to release to others? Why? What do you fear will happen when you share it?

2. Can you identify a time when your reluctance to release has hindered your ability to embrace new possibilities or opportunities?

3. In what areas will you commit to giving more of yourself, gifts, talents or resources?

Day 7 – Letting Go

"Cast all your anxiety on him because he cares for you."
1 Peter 5:7 (NIV)

Growing up, I always wanted my own room. While I did not lack privacy, I simply felt like I never had enough space for my belongings. I specifically wished for a bigger closet—because then we wouldn't have to debate where my shoes or purses, or my abundance of black clothing would find a home.

The interesting fact is, no matter where I lived – with my parents, on campus, or even now at home with my husband – I've continued to find myself making the same wish! Prior to beginning my own journey to be *40 Days Lighter*, I was convinced that the issue was the house, and not my abundance of belongings:

"Well, my sister's stuff took up so much space in the closet at our childhood home."
"Dorm closets aren't really made for decent storage."
"The closet in my room at my parent's new house was just odd-shaped."
"If only the rooms in my home were arranged differently, I'd have so much more space."

Excuses would flow like an unstoppable river!

However, as I experienced the process of decluttering my life, day by day, for the 40 days of the challenge, I was struck by the internal awareness that the act of clearing my space brought. I realized that my issue was not my house or my closet but rather my refusal to **let go** of many of the items I had accumulated, but no longer needed.

I don't think I fully understood the impact that the over-flowing clutter was having on my ability to think, plan, and do, until the moment I experienced the freedom of more space to move. Who knew that my bedroom floor had enough room for a decent workout?!

Then I began to think, and ponder — how much more freedom could I experience in my schedule, relation-ships, studies, and the overall pursuit of my goals if I let go of the clutter overflowing in all areas of my life? What if I could release the non-essential tasks, the forced/unhealthy interactions, the TV/social media/random web-surfing time used to keep me from having to deal with the "important stuff"? What if — and this was a hard realization for me — but, what if I let go of the unrealistic expectations I have for myself and others?

How much easier would I sleep at night?

The truth is that sometimes, we feel that our world, our home, our closet is too small to contain all the "stuff" we've accumulated over the years, when in reality, we are holding onto baggage that we just need to *let go.*

What have you stored up in your emotional closet, what skeletons remain there that need to be swept out, brought into the cleansing rays of the Son-light?

We have become perpetual "bag-ladies," constantly carrying hurts, offenses, disappointments, failures, heartaches and heartbreaks into every new space we are blessed to occupy. Only to find that we are soon dissatisfied and uncomfortable, because there just doesn't seem to be room to store all our junk. I'm here to tell you, there is deliverance in letting go! There is freedom in letting go! Restoration, rejuvenation, and reconciliation can all take place in our lives when we make the decision to just let go!

Letting go doesn't mean that we forget what has taken place.

And if we're honest with God and ourselves, many of us *like* holding on to mementos of times—good and bad—gone by. Why? We use them to hold others captive, to justify our pity parties, to build walls and keep people out, in a bid to hide our heart away, under lock and key, in the center of our dysfunctional fortress.

Instead, real letting go means releasing what has happened to us, or because of us, or in spite of our best efforts, into God's hands, so that He can make something beautiful out of our mess.

Reflect:

1. Identify your baggage: To whom or to what are you holding on, when God is telling you to let go? Are you keeping a record of wrongs or allowing the secrets of your past to hold you in

bondage? Tell God about it. Be open and honest—
remember He already knows your heart.

2. In this technology-driven, social media age, there
   are many more ways to "hold on" to what we
   should let go of. Have you deleted those old pic-
   tures from your phone? Any phone numbers?
   Who do you need to unfollow (and stop cyber
   stalking)? Who do you need to unfriend or even
   block to stop the messages that bring you back
   to your past?

3. Letting go can be hard, so it is always a good idea
   to have an accountability partner or someone
   who can take this "letting go" journey with you.
   Identify one or two people that you can share
   this process with, so that they can support you
   (confidentially) in prayer and encouragement.

Day 8 – Clear It Out: The Process is Worth the Pain!

"See to it that no one falls short of the grace of God
and that no bitter root grows up to cause
trouble and defile many."
Hebrews 12:15 (NIV)

Anyone who has undertaken the task of completely emptying out their closet knows that we all have some items that tend to accumulate in the bottom corners—and might be left for another day—as we do our clean up.

For some of us, it's that box of papers we are "waiting to find time" to sort through and shred. For others, we have those old photos, love notes, and gifts from past relationships, but...nostalgia. Some of us may have shoes that we just love, even though they have done their time. We may have shoes that are beautiful but SO uncomfortable, yet we're reluctant to give them away. Long story short, none of these items are serving us any longer, and simply need to be *cleared out* of our space.

I'll be honest, the prospect of this task tends to overwhelm me, but when I think of the relief that follows and the usable space it will create, it makes the process worth the pain.

During my 40-day journey, I was inspired by conversations with an aunt and a friend to spend some time examining my emotional closet as well. I needed to take time to be still and allow the Lord to sift through my "stuff." Just like those items that accumulated in the dark corners of my closet, most times hidden by hanging clothes or stacked discretely behind objects in use, I had allowed negative emotions, thoughts, and perceptions (of myself and others) to accumulate in my mind and heart. And I figured because they were often on the "back burner" or hidden behind all the other "proper" or "priority" topics of consideration, I let them be, rather than clearing them out.

One interesting ability of our "train of thought" is that as it "chugs" along, it can bring what is hidden in the background of our consciousness to the forefront at the slightest provocation or smallest of triggers. Someone plucks that "last nerve," and suddenly you find yourself spewing all the horrible—sometimes true, sometimes not—things that have been collecting, waiting to overflow into your conscious mind, and ultimately out of your mouth. We unknowingly allowed a "root of bitterness" (Hebrews 12:15) to come up, courtesy of the weeds in the garden of our mind, that have grown unchecked, un-plucked, and uncontrolled.

Like any good gardener, we desire to have our minds clear of negativity so that seeds that have been intentionally planted for our benefit may grow and bear fruit. No good gardener continues to put more seed in the ground, as they watch the unkempt weeds choke out the plants that already exist. You've been trying to step into your purpose, make your passion into a career, take that next leap of faith, and shatter glass ceilings, but you continually feel like something is holding you back. Maybe it's time to check your mind and heart, and clear out the concealed clutter you've been storing for far too long.

Won't you say this prayer with me?

Lord, please weed the garden of my heart and uproot anything that isn't from You. Remove regret, resentment, anger, unforgiveness and bitterness. It's hard to admit that they are still present in my garden, like those hidden items in my closet, but I refuse to ignore it any longer, lest they choke out the good seeds that have been planted and keep me from bearing good fruit. Help me to be honest with You and with myself. Amen.

Reflect:

Today, take some time to symbolically clear out the clutter. Here are some ideas of ways to "clear it out" so that you can live lighter:

1. Delete unnecessary, unwanted or "this was never going to see the light of day" photos from your phone.

2. Review emails and unflag or hit "complete" on emails that were marked important, but were dealt with and left in your "Important" folder. Probably a good idea – this helps the urgent to look...well...urgent.

3. Be intentional with your time, especially first thing in the morning and last thing at night. If you know "he is not the one," then there is no need to text him and wait anxiously for a response that often leads to temporary gratification, but long-term un-fulfillment. **Instead, reserve that time to pray, read, meditate and write before starting anything else for the day.** This has made a HUGE difference in my perspective on my priorities for the day and the attitude with which I approach them.

4. Clean out your wallet. I'm always shocked at how many little pieces of paper can accumulate in such a tiny space. If you're feeling brave, tackle that oversized purse...

Day 9 – Is it in the Right Pile?

"There is a time for everything, and a season for every activity under the heavens..."
"...a time to keep and a time to throw away..."
Ecclesiastes 3:1&6 (NIV)

As I progressed through my 40 Days Lighter journey shared on my blog, I realized that my process for cleaning up and organizing needed an overhaul.

During my efforts to declutter my closet and dresser, I would pull out one item at a time, repeatedly wavering, back and forth, between wanting to keep it or throw it out, based solely on the intrinsic value of the individual item, and not the bigger picture. This internal wrestling with myself became cumbersome, and I finally decided to follow the instructions of decluttering expert, Marie Kondo, and simply pulling everything in the drawers and closet out into the open, covering my bed in clothes and accessories.

Now, with all my belongings in one heap, I formed two far more accurate piles: what I loved and would keep, and what I no longer needed and would remove. That second pile was then split into two more piles—items in excellent condition to be donated, and a "straight to the trash" pile. I would never have guessed the amount of will power it actually takes to properly prioritize one's belongings.

I had jeans that I hadn't worn in years—whether it was because I was too big, or they were too small, no need to point the finger—but I _still_ struggled to put them in the donate or trash pile! I wish that I could say that they were only a size or two away, but I found a pair of jeans that were upwards of 3 sizes from being wearable, so even with my recent weight loss adventure, it would be quite a while before I could even squeeze a leg in them!

I asked myself why it was so difficult to part with items that I was not using, and simply did not need. I came up with a variety of answers: one pair was the most comfortable jeans I had ever owned; another was a design and color that I just have not seen anywhere recently – making it momentarily irreplaceable. I had tops that, if I'm being painfully transparent, were a style that I liked… on other people…but I probably wore once…or would never actually get around to wearing. I realized that sometimes, we wish we could embrace someone else's sense of style—am I right?

As I thought about my reasons for hesitation in parting with my clothes, I realized that these were often the same excuses that sometimes keep us from making transformative decisions in everyday life.

"This role, position, or way of living I currently possess is just so comfortable."
"That's just my style, just the way I am."
– Or the opposite –

"I want to try doing it like 'So and so', because they did it that way and they were successful." Not realizing that another person's style or life will never be the "right fit" for us.

Some of us are afraid to make the difficult decision to let relationships, jobs, and even downright messy and unhealthy situations go because we're afraid we will never find another one like it. Even though that person isn't helping us grow, even though that job is clearly dead end, even if our very future is in jeopardy, we simply can't let it go because it's familiar.

In this season, I am challenging myself, as I encourage you, to make sure that we are properly and prayerfully prioritizing our lives, so that we can be positioned to fulfill our purpose.

Reflect:

1. This is a good time for another decluttering activity. Choose a category of items you have long wanted to clear out in your home, and define your piles. Make sure you sell, donate or throw away what no longer serves a purpose for you.

2. Are there relationships, perspectives, or unrealistic expectations that you have been holding onto, to your detriment? Why is it difficult to let go? Write these down, and ask the Lord to show you how to proceed with moving forward and letting go.

Day 10 – The Freedom of Forgiveness

"Then the master called the servant in. 'You wicked
servant,' he said, 'I canceled all that debt of yours
because you begged me to. Shouldn't you have had
mercy on your fellow servant just as I had on you?'"
Matthew 18:32-33 (NIV)

Until quite recently, I would say that I have held a
warped view of forgiveness, despite my best intentions
to adhere to the instruction of the Bible to forgive others.
I've recited the Lord's Prayer countless times:

"And forgive us our debts, as we also have forgiven our
debtors" (Matthew 6:12, NIV).

Yet even as I prayed these words, I often failed to keep my
end of the bargain. You see, I would ask the Lord to forgive me and release me from the error of my ways while
I neglect releasing the person who caused me to hurt.

The Merriam-Webster Dictionary defines the word *forgive*: "to give up resentment of or claim to requital," "to
cease to feel resentment against (an offender)."[1] I may
not have mentioned the wounding incident in subse-
quent conversations. I more than likely even had cor-
dial, if not friendly conversations with the person who
wronged me. However, one thing was certain, that
brooding, broadening, embittering sentiment of resentment continued to blossom in my heart. This would

---

[1] (Merriam-Webster, Incorporated 2017)

become even more apparent if ever that individual crossed me, or my loved ones, again in the future.

In some cases, I would attempt to mask my inner disapproval for the offender, so as not to disturb the equilibrium of my associated relationships. Yet, I would make no attempt to intentionally engage the person outside of necessary, polite interactions required by socially-accepted rules of etiquette.

However, if true forgiveness requires the release of the person from the debt of their error, cancelling any "payment" owed, then how can I say that I have forgiven while expecting someone to plead for my mercy, or endure the agony of my ongoing displeasure? In such a case, not only am I holding the individual captive to some past mistake or misunderstanding, I am also holding myself hostage in my self-made prison of pettiness. Unknowingly, we design an inescapable cell that we must then share with our offenders for the duration of the sentence we have imposed. And our only way of escape, is to set the other person free.

The true freedom of forgiveness comes in the act of removing the bars we place on our hearts to jail and confine those who we no longer trust to do us good. **To neglect this part of the forgiveness process, is to continue to carry that person with us, despite whatever physical separation we have attempted to put between us and them.**

I am by no means encouraging anyone to serve as a doormat or punching bag for someone determined or habituated to causing harm. However, in addition to creating physical safety, we must protect our hearts by not allowing the offense to take place afresh in our minds and hearts every time the person's name is mentioned. We must free ourselves by releasing those who have hurt us into the hands of the Almighty God, because the truth is that we didn't create them, and in most cases, we can't change them.

I'm so grateful to know that when I go to God in repentance, and earnestly ask His forgiveness for my sins and faults, He bears no resentment in His heart for me. He does not withhold my oxygen for the next day, or stop the beat of my heart when I have wronged Him. Despite the perception of many, God does not hold a grudge; in fact, He lovingly restores me from my fallen condition.

Free those who offend, and you will find yourself free in the end.

Reflect:

1. How do you normally approach the concept of forgiveness? What does your forgiveness look like? Describe it – draw a diagram or write out the steps. Based on this description, can it truly be considered forgiveness?

2. Are there friends, family members, coworkers or acquaintances with whom you have returned to seemingly normal interactions, yet still hold resentment in your heart towards them?

3. Who do you have the most trouble forgiving? Why? Write a prayer to God asking Him to help you in this area, and teach you how to release the individual who has wronged you.

Part III

LAYING DOWN THE WEIGHT

*P*rior to taking my 40-day journey to living lighter, I became intensely and unsettlingly aware of a heaviness I couldn't shake off, in my body, mind, heart and life. I felt weighed down, and struggled to move forward into the next season of my life, despite sensing the blowing and stirring of the winds of change.

The expression "caught between a rock and a hard place" couldn't adequately describe the constricting pressure I felt. I began to see myself as small—and shrinking by the day—in comparison to the magnitude of my life's circumstances. Being a wife, mother, educator, leader, believer, all felt like too big a task for someone as insignificant, undisciplined, and ill-equipped, as I saw myself.

The truth is, I was very right and very wrong, all at the same time.

Absent the presence and leading of God, life is far too hard for us mere mortals. We find ourselves not only daunted, but totally paralyzed by the obstacles and unwelcome surprises life throws our way. On our own, we are constantly seeking affirmation, acceptance, and a place to belong.

However, when we partner with the Creator, relinquishing control of our desires and plans to the All-Seeing and All-Knowing, Sovereign King of Heaven, we find ourselves more than adequately prepared to handle all that life may throw our way. We realize that we have a purpose, and that all our experiences, both good and bad, can and will ultimately be used to make us into the Woman of God we were created to be.

We see pressure then, not as a catastrophic situation from which to escape, but rather, a process used to cause our true beauty, potential, gifts, and identity to shine forth! It is a process used to strip us of the unnecessary, imprisoning, and hindering residue—sin and weight—that keeps us from successfully running our race.

In these next 5 days, we will examine the areas of our lives where our habits have made us heavy, our vices make us vulnerable, and our excuses have eroded our resolve to be all that God has called us to be. We will discover strategies and uncover practical ways to lay down the weight so that we may run our race with patience (Hebrews 12:1).

Day 11 – The Thirst Trap (Drinking Habits)

"Jesus replied, "Anyone who drinks this water will soon become thirsty again. But those who drink the water I give will never be thirsty again."
John 4:13-14 (NLT)

One of the most vital lessons I learned on my journey to living lighter was the importance of drinking water. In Biology class, we learned that the human body is made up of more than 50% water, making it an essential part of our daily food and drink intake.

To say that I have never been very fond of water would be a gross understatement. Since I was a child, I downright hated it. It did not matter how many times I was told it was good for me, that my body needed it, or all the wonderful things it would do for me, I wanted no parts of it.

However, as I embarked on my journey to a healthier lifestyle, trusting the wisdom of my coach, and limited or eliminated my intake of all other liquids, I watched my body visibly change as my water intake increased. I literally watched as blemishes on my skin cleared, my dry, damaged hair began to repair, and a glow that could only be matched by that of my pregnancies returned to my face.

And those were only the external changes! I watched as the number on the scale slowly, but steadily, decreased, jumpstarting my ongoing journey to a healthy weight. As someone who wrestled with infections and kidney concerns, I watched as my doctors—looking for the usual abnormalities in my labs—found absolutely NOTHING.

The issue was not my thirst; as human beings, we are made to experience thirst and hunger, even as a means for mere survival. The problem was with how I chose to satisfy that thirst for most of my 30+ years of life.

In a day and age when phrases like "YOLO" (You Only Live Once), *Just do it*™ (Nike), or *Obey Your Thirst*™ (Sprite) encourage us to pursue our own perception of "the good life," we have become desperately enslaved to our desires.

We seek to fill the emptiness within, to satisfy our longing with momentary pleasures that ultimately leave us thirsty once again, like the water the Samaritan woman went to draw at the well. Yet just as Jesus beckoned to the woman, inviting her into His presence to meet a need, He calls to us today, asking us for room to fill us, all in all, so that we never thirst again! He promises to give us living water that will keep us satisfied, and truly quench our thirst.

Know that your thirst, the longing you feel, the urge to seek and find, the desire to be filled to overflowing, is most certainly from God. It is God's awakening call to us, drawing us closer, so that in His Presence, we can be replenished, nourished...and flourishing.

Reflect:

1. Check and track your daily fluid intake. How are you quenching your thirst – what are you drinking? Are you drinking enough water?

2. Look up the signs of physical dehydration, and write them down. How does this relate to our spiritual or emotional condition? Does any area of your life feel dry and in need of replenishing? Name that area and the "symptoms of dehydration."

3. How have you attempted to quench your spiritual or emotional thirst? Have you found yourself satisfied, or repeatedly seeking another experience to fill you up? Put your thirst before God and ask Him to fill you to overflowing.

Day 12 – Hungry for More
(Eating Habits)

"Blessed are those who hunger and thirst for
righteousness, for they will be filled."
Matthew 5:6 (NIV)

The next major lesson I learned as I made intentional
steps towards a healthier weight and lifestyle, was that
my relationship with food was all out of whack.

As much as I *thought* I had a healthy concept of and
relationship to food, my process to lose weight began
to reveal otherwise. I came to this conclusion as I read
You Are What You Love: The Spiritual Power of Habit by
James K. A. Smith, which is an excellent resource if you
are looking to examine and alter your habits along this
journey.[2] I was introduced to this book at the very beginning stages of my healthy eating journey, so as you can
imagine, I gobbled it up (pun intended).

Intentional reflection on nuggets gleaned from my
reading, meditation, and prayer time revealed a jarring
reality to me — my desire to eat junk was both a cause
and result of my poor eating habits. To break this cycle
of craving, I would need to change the habits that create
the desire. Changing those habits required intense
periods of intentional living, planned grocery shopping,
consistent home cooking, and diligent preparation.

---

[2] This part of my journey was deeply inspired by reflection on the
book *You Are What You Love* by James K. A. Smith.

I found that I needed to change my routines, making a quick stop at Dunkin Donuts, Burger King, or even the local Jamaican restaurant I loved, far more inconvenient and obviously unnecessary.

I knew this was going to be a daunting task. This journey would mean giving up a way of living that had become second nature to me, like breathing air — I want to eat it, I like to eat it, *so I'm going to eat it*. It would mean choosing not to give in to my old eating habits in order to establish new, life-sustaining ones.

I wrestled with myself over the course of a few days, but I ultimately *committed to learning new hungers rather than just satisfying old cravings.*

As I was deeply challenged to develop new tastes, to hunger for the "right" stuff, I found that my old cravings slowly but surely began to dissipate. That brownie that was my "go to" after a hard or emotionally charged day no longer offered that same sense of satisfaction.

I learned that if I ate regular meals, and if my stomach was satisfied with the right foods, there was little room left for unhealthy cravings.

I soon realized that the same process I experienced to change my physical hunger, is the one needed to shift my spiritual hunger as well.

Just as I decluttered my physical diet, I needed to eliminate the distractions in my spiritual diet. I learned to let go of negative, and even poisonous, relationships. I chose not to "feed" my soul on interactions that did not satisfy. A good word from a friend is beautiful, but how much richer are the words that proceed from the mouth of the Creator—words that tell me that I am loved, I am accepted, and I am His.

When our spirits are filled with God's Word, there is no room to receive the negative advances of the enemy, protecting us from embracing damaging perceptions of our identity. Just as our physical body often recovers from illness much faster as our eating habits improve, we will also find ourselves better able to withstand the spiritual attacks of the enemy as we feed our inner being on a consistent diet of Scripture, prayer, worship, spirit-lifting fellowship, and godly relationships.

Reflect:

1. How would you assess your diet: Is it healthy or harmful? If you aren't sure, try tracking your meals for a week. Are you eating more foods that are helpful and good for your body, or is it more junk and sweets?

2. This might be a hard one: Identify an unhealthy eating habit (like eating sweets instead of talking about your feelings, or mindless eating while doing other activities) or unhealthy item in your diet. Commit to cutting out that food or habit for

a specified period of time — try one day, or three days, or if you can, a week or more. Evaluate how your body feels.

3. What is in your spiritual or emotional diet that you know is not good for you? How does it leave you feeling mentally, emotionally, spiritually, and/or relationally? Choose a healthy spiritual habit to replace that negative activity or practice. For example, if you struggle with speaking down to yourself, practice using Scripture to affirm who God says you are.

Day 13 – Training My Heart (Exercise)

"...Throw off your old sinful nature and your former
way of life, which is corrupted by lust and deception.
Instead, let the Spirit renew your thoughts and
attitudes. Put on your new nature, created to be
like God—truly righteous and holy."
Ephesians 4:22-24 (NLT)

About five weeks into my weight-loss journey, I had
dropped ten pounds and lost upwards of three inches
on my waist, which for me was amazing news.

Yet as thrilled as I was about the visible changes, that
excitement couldn't compare with the internal sense of
well-being I experienced because of my changing habits.
My food choices changed, the way I thought about exercise changed, and ultimately my overall perspective on
what it means to be "healthy" changed. It took (what I
initially considered to be extreme) discipline: shopping
for the right things, cooking the right things ahead of
time, waking up early for the gym, and being accountable to my coach and workout partner. And there are
still areas where I am working towards improvement,
like getting enough sleep.

Yet, the undeniable fact remains that my changed habits
changed me, more than in my physique.[3]

---

[3] This part of my journey was also inspired by reflection on the
book *You Are What You Love* by James K. A. Smith.

Just as I was killing my cravings for unhealthy food by eating foods that would nourish me, and drinking water to stay properly hydrated, my heart needed to be fed differently to break the hold of unhealthy desires on my life. My heart needed to be properly watered and refreshed with God's Word. And just like with the health of my body, this re-training of my heart required the fat-burning and muscle-strengthening discomfort of discipline.

Eating and drinking well certainly gave real results in my journey to changing my body. However, it was the discomfort of exercise that began to shape my body. In the same way, our hearts are fed and watered by the Word of God, but we also need the spiritual disciplines like worship, prayer, and fellowship with other believers, among others, to ultimately shape our hearts and lives. *It is through spiritual discipline that the life of Christ begins to form in us!* (One of my favorite resources for more information on spiritual disciplines is the *Spiritual Disciplines Handbook* by Adele Ahlberg Calhoun).

I needed to regularly and consistently make time to spend in God's presence, diligently read and meditate on the Word, be in intentional fellowship with other believers, and choose to live out Christ's love in all my interactions. I had to learn to declutter my lifestyle, eliminating the distractions that kept me from living out the discipline needed to change my heart—just like the junk I chose to leave out of my diet.

I've learned to embrace every and any moment to speak to the Lord and listen to hear what He's saying, like how I sometimes did squats while listening to my class lecture recordings. I learned to pick up my Bible, meditate on the Word, journal, and write more than I reached for my phone to check email or social media.

My heart is still in training, and I look forward to a future where I reflect on this moment in time, and I can see the additional "spiritual weight" that has dropped off me.

My prayer is that you are encouraged to exercise both body and soul, so that your health and beauty will radiate from the inside out.

Reflect:

1. If you haven't already developed a regular exercise regimen, now is as good a time as any to do so. If it's even going for a 30-minute walk each day, our bodies benefit from being in motion. I also found that this is a great time to talk to God. (Of course, speak with your doctor before beginning any exercise plan.)

2. Identify the "junk" or the "fat" — the distractions — that prevent you from developing a disciplined lifestyle. How does this lack of discipline affect you?

3. What areas of your life need strengthening and shaping? Write them down and put them before the Lord in prayer. Seek out fellowship with other believers. Make worship a priority.

Day 14 – Growing Stronger (Building Strength)

But Caleb quieted the people before Moses and said,
"Let us go up at once and occupy it, for we are
well able to overcome it."
Numbers 13:30 (ESV)

It took YEARS to finally arrive at the place where I looked forward to going to the gym. I tried working out during various seasons of my life, even had two gym memberships at one point, but just couldn't wrap my mind around the idea that there was any form of joy to be found in that kind of torture. I saw each trip to the fitness center as punishment – uncomfortable and inconvenient (a nap would have been more appealing) – and reminded me just how much of a fitness failure I was.

Yet if I was going to lay down the weight, something had to give. I was committed to learning to live lighter, so I decided to quit my whining, and using the workout list provided by my coach, I began the difficult process of acclimating myself to a regular exercise routine. And as I followed his instructions, I realized a change began to take place inside of me.

Was working out still uncomfortable?

Absolutely! I still felt the same breathlessness as I attempted to increase my speed and endurance on a treadmill or elliptical. Using weights still put pressure on my muscles and joints. Never mind the soreness that set in after an intense leg day, arm day or back day!

Was it still inconvenient?

Well…if you think getting up before 5am to go the gym, when you have a 5-year-old and 1-year-old, *and* you are still a night owl whose brain thinks you're Einstein right around midnight, is inconvenient, then YES, it was still inconvenient.

Was I still reminded of the fitness journey ahead of me as I worked to reach a healthy weight and achieve the fitness levels/goals I had in mind?

Yes. As a matter of fact, it is still apparent that I have a long road ahead of me as I continue to huff and puff on the treadmill in my best attempt to increase my running time.

What *changed* was my perspective and my attitude towards this journey. I recognized that I was—and still am—a work in progress. I realized my journey would never be finished because I wasn't just working towards "an end;" rather, I wanted God to use this *challenge* to change my life.

I gave in to the stretching and tearing and pushing— gave in to the *discipline* of it all—until one day, I emerged from that season of the journey *stronger*, with more *endurance*, and the ability to *run* with the vision God gave me for my life.

In Numbers 13, what made the difference in the people of Israel's ability to enter the Promised Land, was their choice to see themselves as grasshoppers (verse 33), rather than "well able to overcome it," as Caleb had declared (verse 30). The Israelites needed a change of perspective if they were to embody the strength and courage needed to go in and possess the land. Instead, their aversion to the process kept them out.

It's time to change our perspective, and see our challenge as an opportunity to gain strength.

Reflect:

1. Are you, once again, going through a process that you have attempted before, without previous success?

2. Are you wrestling with the fact that the circumstances—the discomfort, inconvenience, and your overwhelming need to go through the process—are still the same?

3. I dare you to change your perspective. Write down your complaint about your process. And then pray, and write down more positive ways to see challenge ahead.

Day 15 – One Step at a Time (Progress)

"The faithful love of the Lord never ends! His
mercies never cease. Great is his faithfulness;
his mercies begin afresh each morning."
Lamentation 3:22-23 (NLT)

One of the traps I found so easy to fall into on this 40-day journey is the need to get *everything just right,* all at the same time. And if we're being honest, I think we all experience this urge towards perfection at some point or another in our lives.

Yet this need to make life look effortless, or to be flawless in the achievement of our goals, tends to produce a few negative, unwanted results.

First, it left me feeling paralyzed, stuck in a holding pattern of perpetual inaction. I found myself unable… or more accurately, *unwilling* to take the next step forward. Second, it makes all progress, no matter how "celebration-worthy," seem like it's "just not good enough." It limited my ability to see forward movement, in myself, and in those around me.

I had fallen into the trap of perfectionism many times before, which caused me to miss the beauty of the day. As a result, I found myself complaining, moody, and brooding. In order to continue my journey, I had to find ways to regroup and re-focus if I had a particularly off day, or didn't make as much progress as I had hoped in a given week.

One sure way to maintain a positive outlook on life, is to always count your blessings; to acknowledge that, in spite of all the things going wrong in a given moment, there is a whole lot going right.

For me, this meant basking in my children's joy and childlike wonder, no matter the number of misplaced toys. It meant loving on my spouse, even when we don't see eye to eye. It meant being grateful to see another day, even when Murphy's Law seems to be at play. It meant being able to appreciate the multitude of opportunities I had to study, learn and grow, even when the course material and learning process was hard, stretching me in ways I never imagined.

I needed a night to course correct, to get back to center. Rather than throwing my misery into the virtual universe we know social media to be, I took those moments of insecurity to God, and asked Him to renew my mindset. My greatest desire in life is for Christ to be revealed in me, to learn to live and love as He does. I was reminded by a friend that, while we a grow in leaps and bounds in certain areas of life, some changes require us to take "baby steps." They may be the shaky, uncertain, teeter-tottering, duck waddling, toddler kind of movements — but steps forward, nonetheless.

You may have had some bumps along the way, plan A has long gone out the window, and you are way past plan B, C, or D.

Take a moment, refocus, count your blessings, remember how far you have come, and keep putting one foot in front of the other to move forward.

Reflect:

1. How do you respond to your own mistakes or missteps? How do you react when your day is not going as planned? Do you get frustrated, and begin to mentally berate yourself for messing up?

2. How do you appreciate your journey? If you have not done so already, take a moment now to write down some of the changes you have experienced since embarking on this journey.

3. Find three scriptures that speak to you, and encourage you to keep moving, to keep taking steps forward, even when the journey gets hard. To get you started, check out: Philippians 3:13-14, 2 Corinthians 4:16-18.

Part IV

GET YOUR HOUSE IN ORDER

"Give us today our daily bread."
Matthew 6:11 (NIV)

This year, my spring cleaning was well under way long before the actual arrival of spring itself. I was in the process of decluttering my heart, home and life, and it only made sense to take this time to organize the items that would remain, as well as create important routines to help me stay organized.

There have always been so many moving parts to my family's life, and I realized that my previous method of "playing it by ear" was leaving me drained and overwhelmed. It was evident that if I was to have longevity in this journey, each part of my life would need to have "a place" to belong.

The hardest task for me was when my coach asked me to begin scheduling my meals to ensure that I was eating every 2-3 hours, and to plan my meals to ensure I was eating the right foods at each scheduled time. The thought of following through on this one request, was enough to make me consider changing my mind about starting down the weight-loss path altogether.

I'm grateful to have pressed through that intimidating moment. As I followed my meal plan, I realized that this level of organization prevented the day from "happening" to me. There were very few deviations from the plan when all meals were properly prepared, and with me as I went about my day. This also made it harder for me to accept mediocre meal alternatives, as I was now aware of the nutritional value of my meals, and the empty calories that would be consumed if I purchased fast food.

In the same way, developing routines and organizational patterns for our lives and spiritual development that place God in the seat of control, work to bring order to our often-chaotic existence. It brings hope to our uncertain future, and protection against the distractions and disorder of the enemy.

Over the next 5 days, we will discuss the need to put your physical house, space, or habits in order, as well as examine how we ensure that our "spiritual houses" are in order. We will reflect on the necessary routines and meal plans required to ensure regular intake of our "daily bread".

Day 16 – All It Takes is One Choice

"Today I have given you the choice between life and death, between blessings and curses. Now I call on heaven and earth to witness the choice you make. Oh, that you would choose life, so that you and your descendants might live!"
Deuteronomy 30:19 (NLT)

I often find myself looking at my life with almost disbelief. In an incredibly short period of time, my life has changed in ways that I have struggled to make happen for years, to no avail. I began asking myself why I was unsuccessful all those times before and I came to one conclusion: I never decided to make the changes stick.

It's a funny thing; we can be introduced to the best program for weight-loss success, discover a life-changing business opportunity, or find an open door to make our dreams come true. Yet, until we decide that we *want to change*, nothing happens. *Everything remains the same.*

I've tried losing weight for external reasons—to be skinny, or to fit some unreachable, unrealistic beauty standard, or simply because "everyone says you should do it." In truth, even my doctors telling me I needed to lose the weight, for my health's sake, wasn't enough for me to keep up my efforts after losing the first five pounds.

After a few weeks, I would grow tired of the effort it took to continue making the necessary, daily choices to reach my goal. And this lack of conviction was manifesting in other areas of my life as well.

I wanted to write, but couldn't keep up with my blogging after a week or two. I'd quickly scribble down three chapters of a book, but always struggled to go on to chapter 4. I had even set up an entire website to start offering resume writing services, and just couldn't hit publish. And even when I finally published it, I wouldn't share it, and eventually I just took it down.

I had great ideas, but I was yet to decide that I *wanted* to put in the work to make them real.

So, I asked myself: What is different this time around? And I realized that I had arrived at a crossroads with one choice to make:

1. Decide that I was happy with my life—my weight, my health, my work—just the way it was (which would have been a lie).

OR

2. Open myself to embracing a new way of life and change what made me unhappy.

Now, I'm not saying that every unpleasant aspect of our lives can be altered by our individual choices. However, in my own life, I realized that most times, when I am unhappy, I have rarely exhausted all my avenues to making it better. Instead, I'm sitting and sulking and waiting for some external solution that requires little effort on my part!

I refused to choose. I refused to choose action over inaction, trying over fear of failure, faith over doubt, peace over my right to be right, and love over indifference. *And my choice to not choose left me feeling hopeless.*

I'm grateful for the God-ordained conversation and kind words from an old friend that encouraged me to get serious about my life, and make changes. All it took was one choice; and as I now write, I KNOW I made the right choice!

Finally deciding to make intentional moves towards a healthier, refreshed, and decluttered way of living set me on the necessary trajectory to bring to fruition the dreams and visions locked up inside of me.

It took just one choice to use a method unfamiliar to me (at the time)—meal planning, tracking, and scheduling—to lead me to a 20-pound weight loss. It took one choice to declutter my closet, heart, and mind to lead me towards a life lived with room for God to move and breathe in me and order my steps.

It is time to decide.

Reflect:

1. What decision have you been hesitating to make? What has caused you to delay or procrastinate? What is the "worst" that can happen if you decide

to move forward? How will you or the people you care about benefit from this decision?

2. Are you entering or are you currently in a season of life that requires you to embrace a new method or habit? Write down what you find most rewarding or most challenging about adapting to this new way of doing things.

3. What is God saying to you about this decision? Be intentional about seeking the Lord in prayer, and spending quiet time to reflect on His Word. Keep a journal or notebook or use a notes app on your phone to document what you hear.

Day 17 – Turning the Page

"Therefore we do not lose heart. Though outwardly we
are wasting away, yet inwardly we are being renewed
day by day. For our light and momentary troubles
are achieving for us an eternal glory
that far outweighs them all."
2 Corinthians 4:16-17 (NIV)

The day I opened a fresh journal to begin this writing project, I paused for a moment to consider the beauty of that first blank page. Void of ink and covered with inviting lines that seemed to beckon my pen near, the prospect of "starting over" caused a palpable tingle of excitement.

Those empty pages could become anything under the pointed tip of my chosen writing tool, and the influence of Divine inspiration. I only needed to put pen to paper, pressing down ever so carefully to form that first word, and "Tada!"—something new started. Even as I began to join the first few words of this book, like a beautiful pearl necklace being strung together ever so carefully, I had a very limited view of how the final product would look—and even more frightening—how it would be received by others.

Starting over, especially when we have experienced failure in the past can be incredibly overwhelming. We ask ourselves a myriad of questions — Can I do it this time? Do I have what it takes to finish this time? Am I strong enough this time?

We find ourselves vacillating between moments of *Am I good enough?* and *Why do more? I'm good enough right where I am.* We cause our fear of not knowing the outcome to cause us to doubt who God created us to be. We even begin to wonder if we are worthy of the assignment to which we have been called. Let me offer some relief here; God is the only One who is good, and the only One who is worthy. Yet in His love for us, He makes us worthy by the redeeming sacrifice of His Son, Jesus Christ.

When we release ourselves from the burden of making it happen, and instead give our plans to God, we can find the courage to turn the page and start again, no matter how things turned out in the past. Hear the words of the psalmist encouraging us today: "*Commit everything you do to the Lord. Trust him, and he will help you*" (Psalm 37:5, NLT).

2 Corinthians 4:16-17 reminds us that God renews us inwardly, day by day.

Maybe last week's story didn't go exactly as we planned. Maybe we couldn't find a way to mend that relationship a few days ago. Maybe we simply struggled to get through the work week, and are at this very moment dreading that 6am alarm racing towards us, even while sleep eludes us.

I want to encourage you to take heart – tomorrow holds the promise of a fresh start for you.

Reflect:

1. Circle one – How do you handle a day that seems to be filled with defeat?

    a. Do you lay awake, sleepless at night, mentally beating yourself up over mistakes you've made?
    b. Do you spend the time in tears, running through every possible scenario that could have caused a more desirable result?
    c. OR Do you commit the day behind you to God, asking for understanding to learn from your mistakes, forgiveness for your own misguided or disobedient actions, and grace to move forward?

2. Has failure made you afraid to try again? Do a quick search to see what scripture says about failure (Ex: Proverbs 24:16, Psalm 37:23-24, 2 Corinthians 4:8-9). Write it down.

3. Do another search to see what the Bible says about God making things new, and offering new mercies, or another chance to someone who has messed up. (Ex: Psalm 40:2-3, Psalm 145:14, Lamentations 3:22-23, 1 John 1:9).

Day 18 – Love that Lightens the Load

"There is no fear in love. But perfect love drives out
fear, because fear has to do with punishment. The one
who fears is not made perfect in love."
1 John 4:18 (NIV)

Among the most joyous parts of this journey was the
effect that decluttering my physical, mental and emotional space had on the relationships in my life. The
decluttering process brought about a clarity in my heart,
mind, and life that I had struggled to achieve for some
time. It made clear which relationships needed some
work, prioritized the ones that should remain in the
next season of life, and made very apparent those that
were approaching their end.

Specifically, in my marriage, somewhere between saying
"With this ring..." and our 6th anniversary, our relationship seemed to pick up a lot of clutter. From one baby
to grad school, immediately to another baby, to another
job, life's changes had done a number on our relationship compass, and we found ourselves pulling in different directions.

Before we realized what was happening, the clarity
and calm we felt as we said our vows was exchanged
for the burdensome "ball and chain" sentiments. Our
lines of communication got mixed up, resulting in a nev-
er-ending round of "can you hear me now?", seemingly
yelled from one planet to another, existing in 2 different
worlds—under one roof.

As I committed to taking this journey, we both made efforts to declutter our time, reorder our priorities, re-organize our room (it was amazing to have OUR space back), and clear out the backlog of emotional junk we had just been sweeping under the rug over the years. *The result?* We began to experience the return of that sense of clarity and calm we once cherished.

We recommitted to being partners in life, love, and most recently, in losing weight. We are forging ahead into a bright future, our steps surer, and our heads held high, because the burdens of life are lighter when we lift together.

Most remarkably, the restoration of my marriage, solidifying of my friendships, and overall refining of my circle helped to remove the one feeling that holds so many of us back from pursuing the future and life we were created to have — fear.

We are reminded in Scripture that "perfect love casts out fear" (1 John 4:8, ESV). When we fully receive the love of God, and begin to live out that love in our relationships, we will find that we no longer need to carry the burden of fear — of the future, of uncertainty, of being alone, and even the fear of failure. God's unconditional love empowers us to live boldly, and to move confidently towards the destiny He has divinely designed for us.

Reflect:

1. Have you found yourself in a place where your relationships make the road ahead seem dark and daunting, weighing you down in your walk? Or do they make the mountains ahead appear more manageable because you are assured that you aren't going that road alone?

2. If you share your home with your family, or you are in business with a partner, or if you even work on a team at your job, make note of the times when asking for help could have made the difference between success and failure. What stops you from being vulnerable and asking for help OR encourages you to let others in and ask for help?

3. How does your love lighten the load of others? When is the last time you asked, "How can I help?" without expecting anything in return? Make a list of opportunities where you are willing and able to help bear another's burden.

Day 19 – Little by Little

"Little by little I will drive them out before you, until
you have increased enough to take
possession of the land."
Exodus 23:30 (NIV)

Have you ever found a new apartment or moved into a
new home and you can just *see* all the amazing changes
you wanted to make and how beautiful it was going to be?

When my husband purchased the house that would
become our home back in 2009, that's exactly how we
felt. We imagined how we would arrange the rooms, the
paint colors we would change, and the wallpaper we
would take down, removing the previous owner's foot-
print. Of course, as it sometimes happens, we wanted
these changes to happen all at once. We soon realized
that 'all at once' simply would not be feasible based on
our budget and time constraints at that time.

At first, I found myself disappointed—*you mean money
won't fall out of the sky to give me the oversized walk-in
closet I always wanted?* Yet as those feelings quickly
dissipated, I recognized that the process of making this
house our "home" would be part of building our relationship and life together. And along with that change in
perspective, came smaller, practical steps we could take
to eventually bring our vision to fruition.

Fast forward to my 40-day journey, and as I spent time
in prayer and reflection, I noticed that I was struggling

with this same tendency to go after my goals and dreams in big chunks, often resulting in fear, stagnancy, and mental or emotional paralysis. Yet, I noticed that in the times when I intentionally broke down my big objective into smaller, yet equally fulfilling, mini projects, I found the goal more attainable, and the motivation to push through to completion.

So often, we want everything we've waited and hoped for to happen in a single moment, and become disillusioned when this is not the case. We work out and eat healthy for a week, and want to see that we've dropped more than a few inches off our waist in that time. Some of us begin to give up or quit when the process seems to be slow going. For some of us, if we have a goal that looks too big, we don't even bother trying, when the real solution is to find the smaller steps we can take towards that big goal, and get moving.

In Exodus 23:27-31, God shares with the children of Israel His plan to remove their enemies occupying the land they were promised. He lets them know that it won't be an instantaneous transition, because other issues may arise and overwhelm them if He did it all at once. Unfortunately, we know from Scripture that the Israelites didn't trust God enough to take the land the first time around. Yet I'm grateful to know that He give us another chance!

Sometimes God's plan is not an immediate turnaround, but a "little by little" plan. During this season, God changes us as He reveals Himself to us in ways we did not know Him previously. Sometimes He allows transformation to happen little by little, so that we don't pick up more formidable foes. For some of us, if we completed the process all at once, we might fall into pride, self-righteousness, or vanity. For others, based on the way our faith is set up, we might begin to wonder *"Is that it?!"* because it just seemed too easy.

Don't become disheartened or discouraged by the "little by little" processes in your life!

Whatever His reasons, God, in His word to the Israelites, gave us a model we can use when we have an almost insurmountable goal to accomplish, or giant-sized task ahead.

- Depend on God. Trust His heart for you, and understand that His ways are not your own.

- Know that God is the One who gives us the victory. We can't do it by ourselves, but with Him, nothing we do according to His will, is impossible.

- God's promises are sure. Know that He will do exactly what He said, so no matter how long the journey, He will complete the work He started.

Reflect:

1. Name your big goal or goals and write them down. Add detail to your list—for example, by when do

you want to complete them? What resources do you need to get there?

2. Now ask yourself—what can I do, what steps can I take **right now** to get closer to that goal? How much time do I have **right now** to dedicate to the completion of that goal? What can I sacrifice **right now** to make room for or allocate time and resources towards the accomplishment of my goal?

3. What is the goal you gave up on because it was too big? Reflect on the moment you decided to quit. Is there anything you could have done differently? Write that down and commit to approaching your aspirations with a renewed perspective.

Day 20 – Sanity Savers

"Don't worry about anything; instead, pray about
everything. Tell God what you need, and thank him for
all he has done. Then you will experience God's
peace, which exceeds anything we can understand.
His peace will guard your hearts and minds
as you live in Christ Jesus."
Philippians 4:6-7 (NLT)

There is so much that happens in our lives, and in our
world, that is far beyond our control. We live in a time
where heartache, panic, stress, contention, confusion,
anger, and grief have become commonplace. Tragedies
occur in such quick succession, that we rarely have
moment to recover from the shock of one event, before
another takes place. As a result, there are many people
suffering with anxiety, depression, fearfulness, resentment, feelings of powerlessness, and stress-related
illnesses.

It can be tempting to try to figure things out on our own,
to think that "we've got this," without consulting our
Creator first. And when our natural minds are unable
to come up with an adequate solution, we worry about
the outcome or wallow in our failure. We begin to allow
fear and doubt to take root, and see ourselves as small
and incapable, insignificant, and inferior.

In these times, it is most important to remember that
setting our house in order also means recognizing and
remembering who is REALLY in control of our lives. The

only way to stay sane in this crazy world, is to give our entire existence to God.

God wants us to trust Him and depend on Him alone, to give Him everything: our hopes and dreams, doubts and fears, gratitude and worship, needs and shortcomings. Just like everything in our homes has a 'place,' all our thoughts, emotions, and experiences have a place to go—they should be laid down at the feet of Jesus!

Philippians 4:6-7 gives us clear instructions on how to handle *ALL* of life's situations!

1. Wash away your worry in the shower of prayer.
2. Lift your needs up to God's ear.
3. Give God thanks for all He has done.
4. Let God's Peace be your protection.

Maybe you've wondered who else can handle the heavy stuff you've been carrying. Who else can bear these unbearable burdens? Give it to God, today!

You will not lose your mind. God has given us His peace to keep us stable and protected.

Reflect:

1. How do you respond to hard times or challenges in life? Do you worry, pray, or engage in both?

2. What does the Bible say about worrying and being anxious? How does Scripture say we

should respond to the uncertainty or trials of life? (Check out Proverbs 3:5-6, Matthew 6:25-34, John 14:27, Philippians 4:6-7).

3. What kind of attitude should we have, or behavior should we display if we believe that God is in control? Is this your reality? If not, what changes do you need to make?

Part V

TIME WELL SPENT

*I*t is said that one of the greatest deathbed regrets is *not having spent more time pursuing one's dreams.* It is also said that the place possessing the most potential is the cemetery. These statements show that the tendency as human being is to get caught in a cycle of surviving or enduring our everyday lives, rather than striving to thrive.

So many of us grumble as we get up for work, or complain 'jokingly' about our abundance of family duties and the challenges of raising children. We promise ourselves day in and day out that "one of these days," we'll pursue our dreams. We make up ideal condition scenarios – when the kids are grown, when we finally get that promotion, or when we finally arrive at that ever-moving retirement date that only seems to get further away in this economy. We tell ourselves that eventually we will find the time.

Yet for some, that time never comes.

For so long, I lived under the excuse "when I find time..." as if there was some mystical, hidden place, outside of my God-given 24 hours to find another second, minute, or hour. I soon realized the longer I waited to *find time*, the more time I was *losing*. Like so many, I was wasting this precious gift with an expiration date only known by our Creator.

During the next 5 days, we will explore what it means to maximize the time God has given to each of us. We may not know the length and breadth of our lifespan, but we have a life-altering choice to make about how we use these few precious moments.

Day 21 – If It Matters

"Teach us to realize the brevity of life,
so that we may grow in wisdom."
Psalm 90:12 (NLT)

There are no two ways about it. We make room in our lives for the people and things that matter to us.

Our commitment to a person, process, passion or program is most often evidenced by our willingness to make it a priority by giving our time, talent, or treasure. These are the values, interests, and activities for which we will drop everything, and re-direct our attention to ensure that they are adequately addressed.

Conversely, it is also easy to identify the individuals, tasks, and objectives that are of low importance to us, by the sheer number of excuses we will make to get out of expending any energy or resources on them. I have realized that by labeling one thing as important, you automatically infer that something else is less important.

Determining that a task is of low, medium, or high importance is a necessary distinction in our lives, helping us to stay organized and take care of first things first. I mean, who wants to open an email inbox where every message is marked "Urgent"?! However, when it comes to determining how to spend our days in real life, that choice is based how much of ourselves we are willing to give; there is no star symbol to highlight or check box to mark.

How many of us have made statements such as: "God, family, career," or "God, family, church," or "Family first," or "My children come before work"? *Yet, if there was a minute-by-minute, or hour-by-hour log of our actions for the day, our actual time spent may not reflect these mantras.*

Going through this 40-day journey and intentionally documenting my plans, activities, eating and exercise schedules made me incredibly aware of just how much time I have dedicated to everything except the things I deemed important in my life. Even more eye-opening, was observing just how often I used the phrases, *"I just don't have time" or "I just don't have the money" or some other excuse.*

In Psalm 90:10-12, the psalmist expresses his awareness of just how brief a time we have each been given here on earth. He cries out, asking God to show us how to wisely use the time we have been given. Using our lifetime wisely means allowing God to arrange our priorities, and allocate our energy, efforts and resources to the mission of His heart—ultimately reconciling all of creation to Himself.

Reflect:

1. Would the time we commit to our relationship with God, or the uninterrupted, present and device-less moments we spend with our families

and loved ones show just how important these ideals are to us?

2. Do we put far more time and effort into making a living, that we have little to no time or energy left to make a life that honors God and brings us closer to who He is calling us to be?

3. In what areas has your time, energy, or resources been misplaced? Write them down. Ask the Lord to reveal where and how you can and should make the best use of all that you have been given. Write down what you sense God is saying to you in your times of prayer and in His Word.

Day 22 – Call a Time Out!

"Then Jesus said, 'Let's go off by ourselves to a quiet place and rest awhile.' He said this because there were so many people coming and going that Jesus and his apostles didn't even have time to eat."
Mark 6:31 (NLT)

I've never been much of a sports fan, but from time to time, I will sit down and watch a game of basketball or football with my husband. As the game would progress and get more intense, I would notice that there were moments when the coaches would call a time out for a variety of reasons. Sometimes it was because someone was injured, or a rotation of players was needed.

However, the more interesting occasions, for me, were when coaches would use the time out as a moment to regroup. Some coaches would encourage tired but tenacious teams to keep their chins up, and heads in the game. Others would remind players to stick to the plan, because things were going great. And still others would pause to revise their strategy, redirect their energy and mount a stunning comeback.

As mama to an almost 6-year-old and 2-year-old, time out is sometimes employed as means to bring disruptive or unkind behavior to a halt. They are asked to sit quietly and reflect on how the preceding situation could have been handled differently — eliciting responses of "I'll share next time, promise," or "I won't hit again; I'll use my words!"

I will never forget the stressful and trying season in my life that changed everything. I felt like the more I tried to build—with my spouse, for our child, in my education and career—everything was crumbling to dust! At first, I told myself, "This is just one of *those* seasons; it'll be over soon." Yet as I kept pushing forward with what had become a mind-bending status quo, crying every day, feeling inadequate as a wife, mom, full-time employee and MBA student, I pushed so hard, that one day (I believe, anyway), God allowed life to push back!

My Loving, Heavenly Father, put me in a grind-stopping, unexpected time out, bringing every turning wheel in my life to a screeching halt! For four, whole days, I was forced to stay home, and could do little more than talk to God. Well, screaming at God might be a more accurate description.

Day One – my car suddenly wasn't working. *No biggie. Hubby has a car.* Day Two – hubby's car won't start either. *Grit your teeth and call the dealership.* Day Three – the baby is sick. Day Four – I'm sick. *What gives?*

I remember how by Day 4, I had **no** soft, prayerful tone left. I was full on *wailing* at God, tears streaming down my face. And in a moment that will forever remain clear in my mind, as I stood at my kitchen sink, distractedly washing the same plate over and over, I suddenly shut up long enough to hear my Father speak.

And He caused me to remember how I had gotten to this place, living miserable with my life, busy and overwhelmed. He showed me that I had been meditating on the wrong perspective for all these months; and as He gave me a glimpse of His love for me, He gave me strategy for the next season of my family's life. Little did I know, my next move – which was leaving my full-time position in insurance to work part-time in higher education – would be the move that would change my entire career trajectory.

In my mind, those four days of disruption were working against my plans. Yet, I've learned that God's interruptions are used to give our lives direction. Don't resent the times when business as usual is divinely disrupted. Instead, find a space to quiet your spirit, open your heart, and listen for the voice of your Father in Heaven!

Reflect:

1. Has God ever put you on time out? What led to that moment? What was the result of that moment of interruption?

2. Sit very still for a moment. Ask yourself, "Do I need a time out?"

3. When is the last time you've had a strategy re-alignment?

Day 23 – Twenty-Four Seven

"So be careful how you live. Don't live like fools, but
like those who are wise. Make the most of every
opportunity in these evil days. Don't act thoughtlessly,
but understand what the Lord wants you to do."
Ephesians 5:15-17 (NLT)

Without a doubt, we have all been given the same 24
hours in a day and the same 7 days in a week, *whether
we accomplish magnificent feats with our time, or
we waste it.*

The person who finds the cure for cancer, or the one
who develops technology that alters life as we know it,
the woman who writes a NY Times bestselling book, or
the man who leaves a legacy of serving the hungry and
homeless, all have the same number of hours on their
days as we do. And while life experiences, family obliga-
tions, access to education and opportunity, and systemic
inequality do play a role in what we are equipped to do,
the truth is that many of us can admit that we have not
made most of our time.

I periodically think back to my high school and under-
graduate education years, and can distinctly identify
doors of opportunity that I ignored, out of distraction,
disinterest, or plain old ignorance. At my lowest points
in life, such memories would cause me to get stuck in a
spiraling cycle of regret, wondering if I'd waited too long
to pursue my passion, or if my *big moment* had passed,
never to return.

I quickly learned that dwelling in this place only caused me to miss more moments, and become filled with more regret. I also learned that the key to breaking this cycle, is to acknowledge the moment, remember how and why it happened, and determine in my heart not to repeat the pattern again. I learned (the hard way, aka from a broken heart) that I could spend my time endlessly dating, or remain single to work on who I am as a person, so that I can bring something of value to a relationship, beyond my body or beauty. I learned not to turn down an invitation to work on an unfamiliar project, but to be brave and step into the unknown, because my greatest moments of growth would happen in those spaces.

In Ephesians 5, we are reminded to carefully consider how we live, to be wise, and "make the most of every opportunity in these evil days" (Ephesians 5:15-16, NLT). The key to *how* we accomplish wise living is found in verse 17: "Don't act thoughtlessly, but understand what the Lord wants you to do" (Ephesians 5:17, NLT). **Think before you decide, speak, or act. Consult God about every choice, no matter how big or small. Read God's Word to receive timely guidance and divine instruction. Pray always — seek constant communication with God, rather than the occasional check-in. Build relationships with wise and *godly* counselors or mentors. Ask your Good Father in Heaven to send these individuals into your life.**

Today, make a commitment to God, yourself, and the generations to come who need your gifts and contributions to the world. Make a choice that you will not live haphazardly, but *intentionally*, knowing that your life makes a difference.

Reflect:

1. Do you feel like life is just *happening* to you, or do you feel like you are making intentional steps towards becoming the person God has called you to be?

2. Are there goals or dreams in your life that you have not yet started to pursue? Why? Write down one or two steps you can take today to begin to make your dream a reality.

3. Try waking up fifteen minutes before your normal wakeup time for one week. Pray and ask God what He would have you do during each day. Is there anyone He wants you to help, or any way that He desires for you to worship Him and serve others. Write down how you sense God is leading you.

Day 24 – Counting Sheep (Rest)

"On the seventh day God had finished his work of
creation, so he rested from all his work. And God
blessed the seventh day and declared it holy, because
it was the day when he rested from
all his work of creation."
Genesis 2:2-3 (NLT)

Along this journey to becoming 40 days lighter, I genuinely struggled and truthfully felt like an utter failure in two areas: finding *times of rest* and *moments for self-care*.

Like so many, I am constantly on the go. If it's not in the care of our family, then it's for work; if it's not for work, then it's for school. And if it's not for school, then it's for church...and the list goes on. Even when I've attempted to build into my daily schedule moments of downtime or quiet, I always somehow found a way to fill the "gap" with something else.

I would plan to just sit in silence, to relax and write, yet as I was passing the kitchen sink to put down my laptop, I'd have a "let me just do these dishes really quick" moment. Before I knew it, I was sweeping, cooking, checking emails, and doing a host of other tasks not related to my writing. I would lay my babies down for a nap, saying, "This is a good moment for me to rest." Yet before I knew it, I would grab my phone or laptop to take care of *one last thing,* which mysteriously transformed into ten **more** things. And suddenly, the children were awake, blinking at me with those beautiful brown and hazel eyes. And I still hadn't slept a wink.

I had taught myself to see rest or downtime as "optional" — a thing I did when I had taken care of everything else, while simultaneously not taking care of myself.

And eventually I crashed. I became irritable, unfocused, frustrated, overwhelmed, and overall, so tired, it would seep into my bones. I was *forced* to pause, because my body and mind refused to go another step forward without recharging first.

In Genesis 2, we see the God of Creation, Limitless and Eternal, who neither sleeps nor slumbers (Psalm 121), taking His rest after completing His work and calling it good. Yet we struggle, as finite, limited, human beings, in our fast-paced, technology-driven culture, to shut everything down and rest – partly because the world tells us that our work is never done! Society tells us, "If you aren't running yourself ragged being the quintessential stay-at-home mom, wife, blogger, personal chef and housekeeper, or if you aren't in constant pursuit of career success, for more money, more recognition, more titles, then you aren't living up to your potential." *This is a lie.*

Today, let me remind you – ***rest is an immovable part of God's plan for our lives*** – our health, well-being, worship, success, and our planet's sustainability depend on it! God has given us rest for a reason. *Could it be that to* *reject rest, is to see ourselves as wiser than God – since even He has given us a model for work and rest by doing so Himself?*

Reflect:

1. How many hours of rest do you get each night? If you are unsure, track your sleeping habits (what time you go to bed and wake up, how often you wake in the night, etc.), using a regular journal, or an app, like *Fitbit*, *Habit*, or some other health app on your device.

2. Are you getting enough rest? How do you feel first thing in the morning? How do you feel throughout the day? Are you able to focus, think clearly, and make great decisions? How is your mood? How do you feel just before you go to bed?

3. Find passages of Scripture that speak of rest. (Check out: Psalm 4:8, Psalm 37:7, Psalm 127:2, Isaiah 40:28-31). What is God's intention for us where rest is concerned? Have you rejected God's rest?

4. How do you interact with or treat people when you've had a good amount of rest? What about when you haven't had enough rest?

Day 25 – Hitting Refresh

"He gives power to the weak and strength to the
powerless. Even youths will become weak and tired,
and young men will fall in exhaustion. But those who
trust in the Lord will find new strength. They will soar
high on wings like eagles. They will run and not grow
weary. They will walk and not faint."
Isaiah 40:29-31 (NLT)

I have long misunderstood self-care. It sounded like
something a person, who wasn't already busy caring
for others would do. It seemed selfish and self-centered,
and looked almost like an "excuse" for people who just
needed a break from their responsibilities.

I struggled to embrace the concept of self-care, right up
until my body decided to let me know, in no uncertain
terms, that I had gotten the idea desperately wrong. I
became tired, run down, and mentally, physically and
emotionally weary. I became resentful and bitter at
responsibilities I had once taken on with joy. I struggled to enjoy my family; work felt far less fulfilling; and
even ministry activities began to sap my strength, and
fade my creativity.

I knew that something needed to change, but at first, I
thought it was an external issue. I figured maybe it was
the number of meetings I had, or maybe I needed to
participate in more meaningful activities or causes, or
I just needed a different job. I attempted to put everything else first, usually leaving me burning the candle

at both ends, and in the middle, and ultimately, I was nearly burned out. I was tired, constantly getting sick, and in need of a moment to clear my head space.

I found out that I needed the refreshing and renewal that only comes from welcoming God's liberating Presence into those moments, to unburden my tired wings and make me light enough to soar again.

The reality is, without emphasis on bringing ourselves back to an awareness of God as the One who created us and cares for us, all of our so-called self-care efforts are just more busy work. Caring for our mind, bodies, and spirits should not be mere attempts to make ourselves feel better about our flaws or shortcomings, like a manicure or pedicure might be on its own. It's not about finding ways to convince ourselves that we're strong enough to take on life on our own.

True self-care brings us back to the heart of the Lover of our souls, the One who beckons us to enter His rest, and to receive His strength for the journey ahead.

I still struggle to make self-care a regular part of my week or day, because of, well, "the to-do list." Yet I have learned that some days, I need only to listen to the prompting of the Holy Spirit and the rhythm of my body, and leave the list neatly tucked in its place on my night stand, so I can yield to these moments of refreshing.

Reflect:

1. On a scale of 1-5, (where 5 is very well, and 1 is not at all), how well do you practice self-care? Why?

2. What refreshes you and helps you to get going again, especially after a particularly busy or stressful moment or season? How do you maintain a low-stress or stress-free life? Make a list of "relaxing" things to do, take a break, but more than anything, ask God to allow you to experience His renewing strength and show you areas of your life where you need to slow down.

3. If you are struggling with stress, where do you turn for help with managing your stress? When is the last time you spoke with a trusted, wise, (and possibly professional) counselor about ways to alleviate the pressure in your life?

PART VI

RIGHTEOUS BUSINESS

"And what do you benefit if you gain the whole world
but lose your own soul? Is anything
worth more than your soul?"
Mark 8:36-37(NLT)

*W*e live in such a consumer-driven and materi-
alistic society. Advertisements and marketing
campaigns bombard our brains, consciously and subconsciously, with their message of "Buy, buy, buy!" All
attempts are made to convince us that our lives will not
be as full, meaningful, fun, or successful as they could
be, if we don't own the newest, biggest, fastest, trendiest,
costliest, or rarest possessions.

Yet the blame does not lay with the merchants, sales-
people, or marketing executives alone. Instant gratification is the "emotional drive" adding to the efficacy of
such marketing campaigns. We want to "have it all," and
we want it RIGHT NOW! It can be so tempting to seek
out the easiest route to the top of the pyramid or food

chain, stepping on toes, burning bridges, chewing up and spitting out "the competition" on our way.

Still, a quick glance at the news will let us know that there are many rich or wealthy, connected and net-worked, famous or notorious, positioned and powerful people in this world who are truly unhappy, and looking for life's meaning. While professional achievement is of great value, it is not the sum total of our lives, nor does it give us our meaning and worth.

There is a right way and a wrong way to succeed, and we will live with the rewards or consequences of the path we choose to take to accomplish our goals. There will always be some form of personal sacrifice involved in the pursuit of success; whether it is the ethical dilemmas that can result from acting with integrity and honesty, or the conscience-killing compromises that result from wickedly garnered gains.

Over the next five days, we will reaffirm that there is *no* earthly accolade or possession worth the loss of our character, integrity, relationships, *and most importantly, our souls.*

Day 26 – Give an Account

"Young people, it's wonderful to be young! Enjoy every minute of it. Do everything you want to do; take it all in. But remember that you must give an account to God for everything you do."
Ecclesiastes 11:9 (NLT)

When I made the decision to enroll in theological seminary, I experienced one of my deepest moments of personal accountability. During the financial aid application process, prospective students are required to give an account for all the student loan debt they have already accumulated, and give an overview of their plan to pay back the owed money. Sounds simple enough.

As I began to write my letter and outline my debt from previous degrees, as well as my career plans, and thoughts on how I would repay the debt, I became very aware of why it can be so difficult for some of us to "own our stuff" in life. It is difficult to say to oneself, "I have arrived at this place in my life because of *my own choices*," whether good or bad.

Accountability requires honesty with God, the people with whom we share our lives, and ourselves. It can make us feel vulnerable, because it does the opposite of the highlight reels we so often post on social media, filled with good and successful moments, instead, requiring us to name our faults, shortcomings, and weaknesses. Accountability challenges our ego, personal preferences, biases and habits, disabusing of us the notion that we are as wise as it gets, and reminding us that we have more to learn, and room to grow.

Yet accountability is never meant to be a prison. Instead, it is, at times, like the bumper rails that children use in bowling, or at other times like the guard rails that stop a car from falling into a precipice or entering opposing traffic. It keeps our lives from spinning totally out of control.

Accountability reminds us that we do not live solely for ourselves. It is a false comfort to think that we are the only ones affected by our decisions. We are all connected in some way. Our personal eating, spending, sexual, or spiritual habits affect our family members, and even the generations to come will be impacted by our collective choices on how to care for the earth—*so our decisions matter.* Accountability removes the blinders that hinder us from seeing the big picture.

YOLO (You Only Live Once) is quite true (speaking of this earthly life). Yet our words spoken, ideals asserted and passed on, actions taken, and causes supported or ignored will have lasting impact on the world long after we are gone. Even more significant are the eternal implications of our temporal lives. What will our story be when we are called to give our account before God? Will we speak of a life lived full and well, or one filled with missed opportunities, unused or misused potential, and unshared love?

Reflect:

1. Who are your accountability partners? Do you have individuals whom you trust to walk with you through life's seasons? How do they help you to live without blinders or stay focused when distractions come?

2. If you don't have accountability partners, why not? Spending time in prayer and carefully considering your own choices are incredibly important, but having someone to help you keep your word, commitments, and encourage you to achieve new levels in life is also essential. Pray to God about what it means to have an accountability partner, and ask Him to send you wise counselors, mentors and friends! Look up the concept of a "Personal Board of Directors."

3. In what areas are you in need of accountability? What vision or dream have you struggled to bring to life? What commitment have you been unable to keep? How can accountability support you in moving forward?

Day 27 – Unleashed

"Just as the rich rule the poor, so the borrower
is servant to the lender."
Proverbs 22:7 (NLT)

With American student loan debt totals in the trillions across this nation, it is fair to say that our generation has been caught in the grips of modern servitude. We were told that we needed a college or professional level education to get a 'good' job, yet in order to afford the skyrocketing costs of higher education, we were also encouraged to spend money we had not yet earned. Many of us are in relationships with the likes of Sallie Mae, that we simply *cannot wait* to escape.

Added to the burden of student loan debt is the availability of consumer credit cards, which so many of us said were *just for books,* or *just for emergencies*, yet have used them for retail therapy, girl's night out, and trips abroad. And while nothing is wrong with enjoying our lives, and 'treating yourself,' we must ask ourselves if it is worth the long-term impacts unnecessary debt can have on our lives.

As someone who has learned the hard way the amount of diligence, discipline, and dedication it takes to clean up my credit and improve my credit score, I'd say that chaining ourselves to creditors for a momentary pleasure that holds no future value probably isn't worth it. If we are going to enter any kind of 'debt' situation, we should be sure that we are making a worthy investment that will pay off in the years ahead, and have a plan to address and repay that debt one day.

Now the concept of debt, and especially the role of student loans, in the financial health of this generation is far broader than I can address in one day of this devotional. So, I simply want to take a moment to ensure that we have a proper perspective on what Scripture says about debt, as it relates to my own life experiences.

First, God's desire is for us to live a life *unleashed*, being free to walk out the purpose He has for our lives, rather than shackled to debts we will simply pass on to another generation. So often, we confess that "we are the head and not the tail," "we are above and not beneath," "we are lenders and not borrowers," but if we do not practice these confessions in our habits and actions, they mean nothing (Deuteronomy 28:12-13).

Second, please know that if you have found yourself on the wrong end of the debt's leash, you are not alone, your situation is not impossible to change, and there is still hope. In my own ongoing experience, I have truly relied on looking to God in prayer for strategies to help alleviate the burden of debt on my family. I do this by limiting how I spend, as well as finding other divinely inspired opportunities to bring in additional income. I have prayed for the grace to handle difficult conversations with creditors while out of work due to illness, maternity leave, or other circumstances. I have believed

God for favor in unfavorable situations and I can testify that He has come through for me time and time again.

Lastly, while I have often wished that I had done things right, from the very beginning, I understand that the hard lessons in my life can be used to help someone else when I place my experiences in the hands of the One who makes all things new and enables us to redeem the time.

Don't live in regret; instead, make better decisions today for a brighter tomorrow. Consider the cost and make worthy investments in yourself and others.

Reflect:

1. When is the last time you assessed your debt situation or reviewed your credit report? Have you set achievable short and long-term goals for addressing debt, cleaning up your credit or building credit (based on your own situation)?

2. What mistakes have you made in your treatment of credit or accumulation of debt? How did you improve your financial standing? If your situation has not yet improved, have you started taking the necessary steps or reached out to trustworthy counselors for assistance in improving your situation?

3. As you reflect on your spending habits and life-style, begin to write down your areas of incon-sistency, weakness, or lack of discipline. Ask God to give you His perspective on your finances, acknowledging that He is your only Source, and that He has called you to be a faithful steward of the resources He has provided.

Day 28 – Slippery Slopes

"Then he said, 'Beware! Guard against every kind of
greed. Life is not measured by how much you own.'"
Luke 12:15 (NLT)

Drive, ambition, high aspirations, and big dreams all
have their place in our lives. Without a sense of internal
drive, we become lackadaisical and complacent, in need
of some external force to push us along in life. Without
dreams, goals and ambition, we might find ourselves
merely existing, limiting our own potential, suppressing
our gifts, and missing out on the full life we were meant
to live. In short, the desire to have an impact on the
world around us is important.

However, it is also essential to remember that *how* we
achieve success matters just as much as *what* it is we
succeed at. After all, money does not equate to meaning,
power does not equal purpose, and fame and fortune do
not secure one's future.

The hunger for more is a common part of the human
experience, as we find that our flesh is rarely satisfied. We
overeat, oversleep, over-spend, over-consume, and we
are overworked. We have driven various species of plant
and animal wildlife to the brink of extinction because
of our desire for more land space for sprawling cities,
more rare materials to build and decorate our homes,
or more extravagant meals at overpriced restaurants.
The very earth groans at our unending consumption

and forceful stripping of its natural resources to fuel our man-made inventions.

We obtain a title, position, or public recognition, and then use it as a hammer over the heads of those who serve alongside us, hungry for more power, higher position, and increased pay. We are willing to step on, not just the toes, but sometimes the necks of those who have been our partners, supporters, and advocates if it will give us an edge in getting ahead.

We are reminded in Scripture that in the end, the value of our lives is not commensurate with the material gain we accumulate (Luke 12:15). Greed can sometimes be mistaken for mere desire, because it often works slowly, over time. Yet one thing is sure, it continually grows until it becomes a monster we must now defeat. We must be careful that our desire for success, wealth, position or recognition does not cause us to become greedy and lose sight of our purpose.

The true measuring stick of a life well-lived is the quality of our walk and relationship with God. In Luke 12:21, Jesus concludes His story of the rich fool, stating, "Yes, a person is a fool to store up earthly wealth but not have a rich relationship with God" (Luke 12:21, NLT). Verses 22 and 23 go on to tell us, "Then, turning to his disciples, Jesus said, "That is why I tell you not to worry about everyday life—whether you have enough food to eat or enough clothes to wear. For life is more than food, and your body more than clothing" (Luke 12:22-23, NLT).

Don't allow greed to trick you into believing that you can somehow sustain yourself by "getting all you can, and canning all you get," as the saying goes. *The deception of greed is that as it drives you to consume, it also consumes you.* It will steal the true meaning of our lives, chalking our days up to nothing more than a money grab, power struggle, or attempt to fill our bellies with far more than our bodies can handle.

Greed says, "I cannot trust God to supply my needs, so I must store up all I can for today." ***Faith says, "Your life is important to God, and He is committed to your care. Trust Him with your provision."***

Reflect:

1. In what areas do you think people often experience the lure of greed in their life?

2. Can you identify a time in your life when you have wrestled with some form of greed? What effect did it have on your spiritual life, relationships, career, or overall well-being?

3. How do we defeat greed? Look to the Word of God to inform your prayers when you feel your heart is being pulled away from God to pursue other desires. (Check out: Hebrews 13:5, Matthew 6:24, 1 Timothy 6:6-10).

Day 29 – By Any Means Necessary?

"People with integrity walk safely, but those who follow
crooked paths will be exposed."
Proverbs 10:9 (NLT)

Along with avoiding the sin of greed, living lighter in business, our careers, and everyday activities requires honesty and integrity in all our interactions. In a day and time when it seems that there are no absolutes, and our moral values are self-defined, it can be easy to want to validate the unethical actions of people who faced opposition in an unfair system.

On the other hand, when I read of individuals like Joseph and Daniel, who maintained their integrity, moral principles, and reverence for the hand of God on their lives, *amid captivity*, I am encouraged to pursue the righteous path, regardless of the adverse circumstances I face. We read of the excellent spirit Daniel possessed, setting him apart from the other wise men in Babylon (Daniel 5:12; 6:3), and how even Pharaoh, ruler of all Egypt, identified Joseph as a man "so obviously filled with the spirit of God" (Genesis 41:38, NLT).

The lives of these men prove that even those around us, who do not have a relationship with God, can recognize whether we are people of integrity or not, and can clearly identify when God is working through us. The honorable reputation of many impactful men and women throughout history did not come without a price.

For Daniel and Joseph, there were attempts to tarnish their names and defame their character by those who sought to take advantage of their gifts or overtake their position in the kingdom. Yet in the face of adversity, they stood their ground, relying on God to be their defense and deliverer. Both endured ridicule, accusation, imprisonment, and murderous attempts on their very lives.

Scripture lets us know that the choice Daniel and Joseph made to remain true to God in the face of opposition became the key to their redemption. God used the evil plots of the very individuals who conspired against them to not only bring these young men into great positions, but also to judge those who set the snares in the first place.

It may seem like it pays, in the moment, to be dishonest, deceitful, underhanded or unethical however, life will quickly prove that it will cost us so much more than we've gained in the long run! Proverbs 10:9 reminds us that "those who follow crooked paths will be exposed" (Proverbs 10:9, NLT).

Joseph could have slept with Potiphar's wife, and never been discovered. Daniel could have secretly prayed to his God, rather than in the open as he had always done. Both men might have avoided a portion of the heartache they ultimately endured, had they chosen to pursue the path of least resistance or take the easy way out. Yet, they endured hardship, faithfully, and in the end, the sacrifice of their momentary comfort, safety, or position, became the platform on which their legacy would be established. *We can and will choose the ethical, honest, and righteous path when we recognize that it is God who is our defense and protection.*

Reflect:

1. Have you ever faced an ethical dilemma? Or have you ever been in a position where you could do something dishonest and not be found out? How do you respond to these situations?

2. How do you respond to situations where it would be easier to "go with the flow," even though you know that what is happening is wrong? If your response to that situation was to be published in tomorrow's news headlines, would you be proud of your actions or ashamed?

3. How do you find the will to do the right thing, even if no one else around you agrees with you?

Day 30 – What's in Your Hand?

"But Moses protested again, "What if they won't believe
me or listen to me? What if they say, 'The Lord never
appeared to you'?" Then the Lord asked him,
"What is that in your hand?"
"A shepherd's staff," Moses replied."
Exodus 4:1-2 (NLT)

I absolutely love reading about the calling of Moses in
the desert. I so often feel like I can relate to his perspective on his identity and his abilities in that moment.
Moses was still recovering from the shame of having
murdered someone. Regardless of the reason, the guilt
of his actions, and the ensuing confusion about his own
identity left him feeling disqualified for any kind of leadership role.

I would have to write many more books to describe
in detail the many ill-informed and shame-inducing
choices I have made in my own life. And so often, on
the heels of a failure, it became easy to label myself as
unqualified, unworthy, and lacking the proper ability or
gifting to do or be anything useful in the future. Like
Moses, I have been tempted to allow the shortcomings
of my past to discredit the value of my future.

*What if they hear about my past? What if they don't
believe You called me? What if they don't like my ideas?
What if I'm not strong enough, smart enough, experienced enough? What does little ole me honestly have to
offer anyone?*

We must understand that God sees beyond who we have been, how we have failed, and even beyond what we haven't accomplished yet. God can take even the things that we have discounted and devalued in our lives, because of our experiences, and use them to accomplish great things for His Kingdom. God asked Moses what he was holding in his hand, and all Moses saw in that moment was a shepherd's staff (Exodus 4:2). *It's just a staff. It's just some writing. It's just a song. I just cook. It's nothing, no big deal.* Sounds like so many of us!

I sometimes wonder, what would have happened if Esther had said, "I'm just a queen, how can I help my people?" (Esther 4). What if Ruth decided she was just a young, childless widow, who might as well go home (Ruth 1), or if Mary said, "I'm nothing but a young girl, so how can I carry and care for the Son of God? (Luke 1).

God used the staff in Moses' hand to do wonders in Egypt, and even part the Red Sea (Exodus 7-14). The prophet Elisha instructed a widow to use the little oil she had left to pay off her dead husband's debts and provide a future for her sons and herself (2 Kings 4). Jesus used a little boy's lunch to feed a multitude (John 6), and uneducated fisher men to change the world (Acts 4).

Your life has purpose! History needs YOU. God can use the very thing you feel holds little or no value and change the trajectory of your life, family, community, and generation!

Reflect:

1. What ability, talent or gift have you devalued or discredited in your life? What is that secret passion you have that you have yet to share with the world for fear of how it will be received?

2. Is there any area of financial need in your life? Are you lacking opportunities in your current position to develop and make a difference with your gifts? What do you have that you can use to start a business or give back to your community?

3. What has God revealed to you that you can use to change someone's life? Have you acted on those instructions yet? What is holding you back? Ask God for strategy to overcome that internal or external obstacle.

Part VII

PREPARATION & PURSUIT

*E*verything that has happened in your life up to this point has a part to play on preparing you for your future. The lessons learned, losses mourned, achievements gained, and battles won reveal more than mere history. If you look carefully, and listen keenly to God's Word to your heart, you will notice that God has allowed all parts of your life to reveal not only who you are but more importantly, *Who He Is.*

Every storm I have endured has prepared me to see God as my Refuge, Shelter, and Peace during the storm. Every fight lost, or victory won, has revealed to me the One who is Mighty in battle, who fights for me, and that my greatest triumphs come as I depend on His Strength and not my own.

In sickness, I came to know God as my Healer; in health, I learned He is my Sustainer. In lack, I found out He was and is my Source; in plenty, I got to know the God of the "exceedingly" and "abundantly" (Ephesians 3:20). In brokenness, He is my Restorer. In wholeness, I can testify that He is my Shalom.

As I continued to reflect on my life's journey thus far, I realized that if each new day is a fresh opportunity to get to know God in a different way, then every day matters. And knowing that every day matters, means there is no room to live for the weekend, or for 'someday' or 'one day.' How we prepare for and pursue the future is just as important as the incredible future that awaits us.

Over the next five days, we will examine our mindsets and perspective towards the future. We will be encouraged to act now, get our priorities straight, and walk out our why, knowing that we have been graced for the journey ahead.

Day 31 – I've Been Meaning to...

> "We must quickly carry out the tasks assigned us by
> the one who sent us. The night is coming,
> and then no one can work."
> John 9:4 (NLT)

"I've been meaning to..."
"You know, I really should..."
"Someday I will..."

These are statements that I've used so many times in my life that I'd be filthy rich if I had a dollar for every instance.

I believe it is fair to say that we create some of the clutter in our lives. Every time we have a dream, vision, goal, or simply a tedious but necessary task that we decide to put off, and saying we'll get to it "eventually," we banish our dreams to the land of "never". We cast something precious into an overflowing pile of unfinished business.

I have long left a trail of dropped dreams, abandoned visions, and forgotten possibilities. As I assessed the areas of clutter in my life, this inability to finish what I started came up for review. It put a glaring spotlight on what has kept me from holding on to my dreams, goals and visions with a tighter grip.

What I found is that I was cunningly comforted by the lie of "later." *Later* goes by different names, depending on who you ask. Some of us know it as "Next Time," "Tomorrow," or "Someday." Later is like that friend that always says, "I'll be there," but never actually shows up.

Later holds a promise of fulfillment, yet often leads to disappointment. Later is married to Procrastination who gives birth to Frustration, Failure and Fear.

(Please note that I am not referring to waiting patiently, especially on God and His timing.)

I am talking about the conscious decision we make to intentionally delay action, because we think that a more "convenient" moment awaits us—not a more appropriate moment, not even a more meaningful moment, but a more convenient one. And if there is anything I've learned about procrastination, *it ONLY leads to inconvenience.* If we are always waiting for "later," we will miss the blessing and miracle of NOW.

We must commit to dealing with the unfinished business that has accumulated in our lives, stifling our inspiration, killing our creativity, and inserting doubt in even the most well-thought-out ideas. I had to give up my life of litter—dropping things I've started, but not completed, all over the place, before they even had a chance to take their proper shape, making them nothing but junk.

There are books to be written and songs to be sung. No longer can we sit in silence, when our voices long to be heard, and there is an audience straining to hear our sound; waiting for the wisdom of the words that we have been given to speak into lives in transition. We can no longer suppress the dance that fills our feet in praise, worship, and adoration of the One who created us for His glory.

It's time for us to try, and it's time for us produce. Let's get moving, finish what we started, and bear the good fruit of a life lived 40 Days Lighter.

Reflect:

1. What are you afraid to try? What scares you most? Is it the possibility of failure or the possibility of success?

2. What is the dream or vision that God has placed in your heart, that you have been reluctant or hesitant to start? What do you feel you need to get started? What are you waiting on?

3. Make a list and write down the plans and projects that you have started, but are yet to complete. Why did you stop in the first place? Is it a God idea or just something you want? If you believe this dream is from God, how can you get going again?

Day 32 – In the Right Order

"Seek the Kingdom of God above all else, and live righteously, and he will give you everything you need."
Matthew 6:33 (NLT)

The path that led to this journey of getting rid of the clutter, and putting what remains in the "right" order, was forged by desperate moments of introspection and prayer where I felt that I had lost sight of my mission. My priorities were getting mixed up and my heart seemed to be splitting into pieces, like glass on the verge of shattering.

My plate was full and overflowing, and I was slowly beginning to realize that maybe like a bad visit to the buffet, I had filled it with all the wrong stuff. What was I doing just to please other people? What was I keeping my grip on, instead of delegating or passing the baton, because of my ego? Even more detrimental, what was I refusing to release, even though the Lord instructed me to let it go, out of a sense of dependence on that resource, rather than relying on God as my Source?

As I began to make my way through this process of releasing the unnecessary, I recognized that due to my failure to properly prioritize, activities that were otherwise 'good' had become unbearable burdens. I needed to return to my First Love, make the 'main thing' the main thing again, and allow God to order my steps and my life again.

We often find ourselves busy, but unproductive. We become like an apple tree that appears to be growing, yet something isn't quite right—it's full of leaves, yet unfruitful. To others, on the outside, it may appear that life is really moving for us because we're always on our hustle or always grinding. Yet inside, we know that we are drying up and withering away; lots of drive, but getting nowhere; #TeamNoSleep, without anything to give purpose and reason to our lack of rest.

It often feels like we will never get ahead if we aren't moving. However, I would like to suggest that if we took time to be still and seek God and the things of God first, we would obtain everything we need. In His Presence, we find the peace, joy, direction, insight, wisdom, innovation, and creativity we need to complete our assignment here on earth. Without Him, we will wander aimlessly through life, no matter how many good ideas we have, or how many opportunities come our way.

When our physical body is out of alignment, when joints, ligaments and bones are not sitting in their proper position, it can cause severe pain, reduced range of motion, and in some cases, the inability to move. The same is true in our lives. If the foundation of all that we do is not the Word and will of God, if we are not seeking Him first, we will experience the same discomfort in our lives.

If you have somehow arrived at a place where all of life seems out of sync, in need of serious alignment, and causing you pain and discomfort, to the point of near paralysis, then it's time to declutter. It's time to put things in the right order, whatever that looks like for you.

Reflect:

1. Find some quiet time with God, and ask your-self if your life is in the right order, prioritized in alignment with His Word and will for your life. If the answer is No, write down how you know that. What are the symptoms? What are the causes? If the answer is Yes, do the same. How do you know and what does that alignment look like?

2. Make a diagram that represents the many hats you wear. Identify your roles and responsibil-ities, whether it is self-imposed, or a duty to family, work, church, community, etc. Be sure to examine your daily schedule and how you spend your time.

3. Now, get a few different color highlighter or markers to color code your priorities, selecting a color ranging from most important to least important. Where does seeking and spending time with God fall? Family? Your dreams? Career? If you find that life is out of alignment and in the wrong order, put this before God and ask for His wisdom in restructuring your priorities.

Day 33 – Inked

"This is the new covenant I will make with my people
on that day, says the Lord: I will put my laws in their
hearts, and I will write them on their minds."
Hebrews 10:16 (NLT)

"I'll pencil you in."

This phrase, so often used by busy professionals and
entrepreneurs, has become a staple in our everyday
conversations. There is no longer time to write a letter,
so we send a quick text to assuage the guilt threatening
to rise from not checking on loved ones. We schedule—
or attempt to schedule—*everything*.

No longer reserved for doctor's visits or formal meetings, we "find a spot" on our calendar for family and
friends alike. We pencil in time with our significant
other, and event with ourselves. And if we are totally
honest, we pencil in time with God as well.

The problem is, a penciled in appointment can be erased!
Anything penciled in is negotiable, removable, and can
be rescheduled or cancelled altogether. I have found,
on my journey with God, that missing my quiet time
with my Creator, who made me and knows what the day
ahead holds for me, brings chaos to the rest of my day.

How many times have we woken up, and after giving
the Lord a quick 'Hello and Thank You,' we set about
checking emails, social media and our calendars for the

day? We remember every reason we wanted to get into the office early, or that project that just needs a "quick finishing touch," or that phone call that can't wait for our arrival at our desk to be returned. And before we know it, feelings of anxiety, insecurity, frustration, irritation, and that nagging sense that you just want to go back to bed to begin to creep in.

I've penciled in and erased the only appointment that causes the rest of the day's itinerary to make sense—time with God. In my time with Him, I am given my marching orders, and a glimpse of how God will be glorified in my life. In this time, He causes my heart to be open to hear His Voice, no matter what transpires during my day. He makes me sensitive to the needs and motives of others—insight otherwise hidden to me, except for the revelation of the Holy Spirit.

We should never be "finding time" to spend with God. Like a tattoo, inked on skin, destined to remain in place, keeping our time with God as a priority helps to create order in the rest of our lives.

We can have busy days, living unfulfilled, and spent following our own agenda, *OR* productive days, filled with purpose, led and directed by God, for whom nothing in our day is too heavy.

Reflect:

1. Examine your planned schedule and actual activities for the last week or month. Has God been penciled in or INKED in?

2. Is there a time that you set aside to read God's Word and other books that build your faith, and pray? When, and how do you prepare for that time?

3. Do you have busy days or productive days? Are you unfulfilled or filled with purpose? If you long to be filled with purpose, ask God to take control over your days. Yield your calendar, schedule and plans to God.

Day 34 – Walking Out My WHY

"He went on a little farther and bowed with his face
to the ground, praying, 'My Father! If it is possible, let
this cup of suffering be taken away from me. Yet I want
your will to be done, not mine.'"
Matthew 26:39 (NLT)

At some point along this path, we all need to be reminded why we do what we do, and re-focus on what our life's journey is all about. One day, after a deeply introspective conversation with a friend, where I reminded her that obedience, not perfection, was the prerequisite to fulfilling her purpose, I felt the need to take my own advice.

Throughout this journey, my coach, mentors, and friends reminded me to "know my why" or "remember my why" or to "work my why." At first, I wasn't sure why this message kept making its way to me, but while I continued through this transformation process, I soon understood.

It became so easy to get hung up on the inches left to lose or pounds left to drop. It was easy to get so carried away with decluttering and organizing my house, that I don't leave room for ordinary living. I wasn't leaving room for my little boys who often played with dinosaurs on my living room floor, or for a tired husband who happened to put his shoes to the side of the couch instead of on the shoe stand, or even for a tired mama—aka me—to get rest instead of stressing about all the things to be done. I was losing focus on my Why.

I forgot to remember that ultimately, this journey was about making room for God to be glorified in my life – by my health, care for my family, friends, or loved ones, and in my ministry or professional endeavors.

I needed to be reminded that this journey wasn't about changing anyone but the person staring back at me in the mirror, to see her smile wider, laugh louder, love harder, and live longer. The aim wasn't to make me a model, but rather, an available vessel in God's hands.

Jesus was well acquainted with the internal wrestling, between self-preservation and serving a higher purpose or the greater good. He knew what it was like to look struggle and suffering in the face, and despite the instinct of His flesh to want to look away, to avoid the trial, He remembered His WHY in the Garden of Gethsemane.

He didn't get lost in Judas's betrayal, the Pharisees' and Sadducees' persecution, or even His disciples sleeping when He asked them to watch and pray. He remembered that He did not come to serve Himself, and humbly yielded His flesh and His will to the Will of His Father.

Walking out your WHY means *worshipping* during your test, *heeding* God's Word, and *yielding* to God's plan for His people and your life as one of His precious children.

Ultimately, this journey is about giving *up* what weighs us *down*, and giving *in* to God's will so that we can give *out* His love.

Reflect:

1. What is your WHY? What lead you to taking this journey, and what do you expect in the end? Write your WHY down and put it up somewhere you can easily see it each day.

2. Have you had moments when you can't remember why you've embarked on this journey or decided to make a change? How do you remind yourself of what matters most?

Day 35 – Grace for the Journey

"For the Lord God is our sun and our shield. He gives us grace and glory. The Lord will withhold no good thing from those who do what is right."
Psalm 84:11 (NLT)

I pray that as you have continued on this path towards a decluttered life that you have taken a moment to appreciate your progress, and recognize the importance of celebrating change, even in small increments.

This mission to lighten the load we carry through life isn't without hiccups and challenges. We face setbacks and delays that are simply beyond our control. As mama to two little boys, I have breathed a sigh of relief after cleaning up all the toys in the living room, only to have another set magically appear, with no idea as to where my children stashed them. Or my husband and I might plan a highly anticipated date night, only to have our plans thwarted by a little one feeling a bit yucky.

Maybe you have worked hard in your studies, only to have one assignment or course come along and do a bit of damage to your GPA. Or you have made great progress in your mission to get active, healthy, and strong, but an unexpected injury significantly slows or seemingly derails your progress.

It is in these moments that you must remember that you have been graced for this journey. God is our sun giving light to the dark places of life and creation, and illuminating the way our feet must go. He is our shield covering us, protecting us, defending us as we face the adversaries that come our way. Obstacles may await us as we move towards our destiny, but we are reminded that God has given us grace for our path ahead. He has promised us His provision as we live righteous lives before Him.

Taking time to declutter our minds, pushing away the thoughts that try to creep in, telling us that "the change won't last", or that "I won't make real progress", is important to strengthening our resolve to keep moving forward. Celebrating our successes allows us to remember how we reached this point, and brings us back to God who has given us grace for this journey, and walks *with* us. We do not walk this road alone.

This 40-day journey is not solely about how your body, your home, or your schedule are changing as you declutter. This journey is also most wonderfully about the transformation taking place ***within you*** as you walk with God through this process.

Reflect:

1. Have you faced a challenge on this journey that has made you feel as though the road ahead is too rocky to continue, or that you are not 'good enough' to complete this process? What was the obstacle? Why did it seem so difficult?

2. Find and write down passages of Scripture that speak to our ability to get past the hiccups and challenges of life with God's help. (Check out: Hebrews 12:1-2, Philippians 3:13-14, Galatians 6:9)

Part VIII

IN HIS HANDS

"Our lives are in his hands,
and he keeps our feet from stumbling."
Psalm 66:9 (NLT)

*A*s we approach the last 5 days of this 40-day journey to lighter living, it is imperative that our goals, plans, and dreams be placed in the hands of our Creator. Our human effort, no matter how diligent and disciplined, is ineffective without God's power to 'keep us from falling" (Jude 1:24).

We've meditated on God's Word, meal-planned, exercised, decluttered, and pursued our purpose, yet here is where we must pause to recognize our helplessness without God's guidance. We are finite beings with limited vision, as it relates to seeing what the future holds. So, what better way is there to secure our future than to commit it to the All-Seeing, All-Knowing, Almighty King of Heaven and Earth – who also desires to reign and rule in our hearts?

In God, we have no need to fear what tomorrow holds. We can live lighter by unburdening ourselves of the worry and doubt that attempt to creep into our minds and hearts when faced with the "unknown." What great reassurance we find when we consider the fact that the One who holds the entire world in His hands, also thought it important to hold my life — and YOURS — in His hands as well.

We are His greatest masterpiece, created in His image, for His glory – *and He CARES for us*. He has even numbered the very hairs on our head, according to Luke 12:7. Today, hear Jesus speak,

"What is the price of five sparrows—two copper coins? Yet God does not forget a single one of them. And the very hairs on your head are all numbered. So don't be afraid; you are more valuable to God than a whole flock of sparrows."
Luke 12:6-7 (NLT)

If we are to resist the temptation to let life burden and weary us more than at the start of this journey, then we must place every moment from this point forward in the hands of the Master.

Over the next 5 days, we will examine what it means to commit our lives into God's hands, find our identity in Him, and yield to His Sovereign plans for our future.

"To him who is able to keep you from stumbling and to present you before his glorious presence without fault and with great joy— to the only God our

Savior be glory, majesty, power and authority, through
Jesus Christ our Lord, before all ages,
now and forevermore! Amen."
Jude 1:24-25 (NIV)

Day 36 – I Am...

"You are royal priests, a holy nation, God's very own
possession. As a result, you can show others the
goodness of God, for he called you out of the darkness
into his wonderful light."
1 Peter 2:9 (NLT)

Near the end of my own 40-day journey, I attended a
birthday paint party where I was asked to choose words
or adjectives to describe who I am, and paint them on
a canvas. I paused to reflect, just for a moment, before
slowly shaping the first letter of my first word — Brave.

Once upon a time, that moment of hesitation would have
come because I had no clue how to describe myself. I
would have sat there, experiencing an existential crisis,
rather than having fun, and celebrating another year
of life for our sister we loved so dearly. In my past,
what should have been a project of passion, complete
with exclamations of "Yes Girl!", "You go girl!", would
have come to an abrupt, tear-filled end, because of my
inability to express my value.

But not this time. No, this time, I was painting lighter.
My mind was decluttered of the negative self-image and
harmful self-perceptions that had so clouded my judg-
ment over the months and years preceding this 40-day
journey. That day, I found the volume turned all the way
down on the noise and chatter of social media, insecurity, and self-doubt. That day, I realized that I was able
to intentionally tune out any other voice except that of

my Creator, my loved ones and myself. I acknowledged, that though I am a flawed human being, I have greatness inside of me as well.

That night, I painted with confidence. My mind was free of the clutter of labels and definitions and "default roles," that I had neither chosen nor desired for myself. And with each brush stroke, I answered the simple question: Who Am I?

My answer: *Smart, Wise, Serious, Kind, Bold, Creative, Savvy, and Strong* (and the list goes on).

More than anything, I realized my identity is found in God, not in my being overweight or getting skinny, not in the multitude of hats I wore, and certainly not in all the "things" I possessed. Our identity is found in Christ alone. We are called, chosen, peculiar, royal, and holy (separated to His service) (1 Peter 2:9). We are children of the King, redeemed, restored, and reconciled to our Father in Heaven.

Today, if you find yourself unable to identify who you are, then it's time to turn down the noise, remove the mental clutter, clear your headspace, breathe deeply, and accept who God has called you to be.

Reflect:

1. When faced with the need to describe yourself, do you struggle to find the right words? Are there negative descriptions that seem to bubble to

the surface? Write down your negative self-perceptions, and then write down the verses of Scripture that cancel out that lie. (Genesis 1:27, Psalm 139:14, Ephesians 1:3-6, 1 Peter 2:9, are great places to start).

2. Have others labeled you in negative, harmful or hurtful ways? Have you resisted those labels, or did you find that you subconsciously lived up to them? Seek God in prayer and reading His Word, and write down what HE says about you.

3. What negative words have you spoken over others? Commit to praying for those individuals, and begin to call them by who God says they are.

Day 37 – PUSH Through It

"As Jesus went with him, he was surrounded by the crowds. A woman in the crowd had suffered for twelve years with constant bleeding, and she could find no cure. Coming up behind Jesus, she touched the fringe of his robe. Immediately, the bleeding stopped."
Luke 8:42-44 (NLT)

Have you ever watched a toddler who really wants something, maybe a toy, or better yet, something they shouldn't have, like a pen? If you have, then you'll have noticed that they are unbelievably persistent, especially when they think no one is watching.

My two-year-old will stop at absolutely nothing, and I mean nothing, to reach my books and pens when he sees any possibility that they might be within reach. He has been known to go and find the seat for his toy keyboard, some cushions to make a fluffy tower, or even a pile of stuffed animals — anything he can use to get a boost — and reach his target. And once he has that pen in his hand, there is no question about what he should be doing with it. As far as he is concerned, any light-colored wall in this house is a blank canvas, and fair game for his artwork.

Terrible two's or not, there is a lesson to be learned from the tenacity of toddlers. They don't know when something is "too hard," and they don't know what it means to hold back. They fully love, hug and snuggle, or fully throw a tantrum. They love a certain food today, and demonstrate their absolute disdain for the same food tomorrow. Toddlers are ALL IN when it comes to life.

As I contemplated our son's "artwork" one evening, I surprisingly found myself encouraged by the message in the mess. I was inspired to approach challenges with a "make it happen attitude," even if it took a million "stuffed animals" to get enough leverage to reach my goal. I was reminded that sometimes the difference between failure and success is laser-like focus – being unconcerned about what others "in the room" are doing, fixing my gaze on the prize and not the distractions. I was encouraged to push through the moments when my goals feel too far away, when I feel like there is too much weight left to lose, or too much work to be done.

In Luke 8, we see this hemorrhaging woman who had suffered for 12 years, without finding relief or remedy for her condition. Yet when she became aware of the presence of the One who possessed healing power, she pushed past her sickness, pressed her way through the crowd, and moved beyond the confines of tradition to get to Jesus.

So often, we allow our condition, our tradition, or our position in society to limit our potential and hinder our pursuit of purpose. However, I believe that if we can find the faith and will power – moved and motivated by the Word and will of God – to push past the situations that seek to confine us, we will find there is healing and restoration in His Presence.

Reflect:

1. What situations or conditions have limited your ability to reach your goals? Write them down, and bring them to God in prayer. Ask Him for the strength to push through, and to begin to see an alternate solution.

2. Does the journey ahead look daunting and discouraging? Have you tried and failed, and now live afraid to try again? I dare you to get up, get in God's Presence, and ***try again***. Failure doesn't have to have the final say.

3. Have others discouraged you from moving forward, whether by their action or inaction? Have you felt "crowded out" of your promise? Maybe you feel like there are already too many people in that genre, platform, or area of expertise. Know that God has made you unique, look to Him for insight, innovation and imagination that will set you apart.

Day 38 – Staying Inspired

"And I am certain that God, who began the good work within you, will continue his work until it is finally finished on the day when Christ Jesus returns."
Philippians 1:6 (NLT)

When you arrive at the conclusion of one chapter in your life, it is important to identify ways to keep up the momentum in the next season of life. I found myself pondering practical ways to continue to live out the lessons I learned, and to maintain the changes made in my habits, lifestyle, and thinking.

I was privileged to have an amazing coach who provided guidance on improving my physical health and encouraged me on my fitness journey. I gained two committed and inspiring workout partners, who I'm honored to also call my family. They continue to challenge me to achieve new levels of fitness. My husband and I are now on this weight loss and decluttering journey together, and I look forward to seeing how our love continues to grow and blossom in this season. I am abundantly blessed to have had a multitude of mentors, dear friends, fellow sojourners, and supportive onlookers to encourage me, uplift me, and push me to become my best self.

Yet, the truth is, the only inspiration that will make a difference, *the only motivation that will last, is what comes from within.* To continue to see positive movement and change requires our own belief and resolve that we can continue down the path we have chosen. We must have faith that God who started His work in us will complete it (Philippians 1:6, NLT). We must decide that our lives will never be the same as it was prior to the start of this journey.

So how can we stay inspired on this journey?

Well, these are the promises that I made to myself:

I will continue to affirm who I am in God, searching His Word, and seeking His face to find out what HE has to say about me; and then I will repeat those words to myself, especially on days when the road gets rough, the sun won't shine, and all I really want is a pity party with some cake.

I will be an intentional participant in relationships that encourage accountability and community, not just to receive wisdom and encouragement, but also to give it, because there is always someone who needs what I have.

I will tell my story, without shame or regret. I will celebrate the changes that have taken place in my life without beating myself up that I did not make them sooner.

I will treat this body as the most expensive, valuable, and irreplaceable asset I own because it is. I will make sure that the care I give to it reflects the care that my Creator has for me. I will care for others because I've learned how precious we all are in God's sight.

I will choose the meaningful and the necessary over the cumbersome clutter.

Reflect:

1. Write down your own affirmations and commitments to this journey—on notecards, post-its or colorful pieces of paper—and put them up in a space that you often use or where you have a moment alone. Make it somewhere that you won't miss. Read these statements out loud every day, until it becomes a part of you!

2. Reflect on the connections you've made or community you've joined along this journey. Identify your "tribe," and commit to living in authentic, accountable relationships that will help you sustain the change.

3. When needed, revisit your written reflections through the course of this journey. Remember how far you have come, and find encouragement for the journey ahead.

Day 39 – Living Lighter

"Then he said to me, "Speak a prophetic message to these bones and say, 'Dry bones, listen to the word of the Lord! This is what the Sovereign Lord says: Look! I am going to put breath into you and make you live again! I will put flesh and muscles on you and cover you with skin. I will put breath into you, and you will come to life. Then you will know that I am the Lord.'""
Ezekiel 37:4-5 (NLT)

LIVE! If there is only one exhortation or prophetic word I can offer you in this book, it is summed up in this one word. *Live* – with meaning, purpose, intentionality and passion.

However, as anyone who has undergone any significant lifestyle change will tell you, you must have a plan to sustain the change. Whether you have battled addiction or dramatically altered your relationship with food, it takes the repeated making of intentional decisions to avoid being caught in the grip of that bondage once again.

You celebrate each small step, counting the days of sobriety, or tracking healthy meal after healthy meal, and properly allocating for a "treat meal" without falling off the wagon. You understand that to actually live your best life, you must daily choose life-giving actions!

Nearly 7 years ago, when I moved from my parent's home into my new house with my husband, I spent an incredible amount of time getting rid of belongings I no longer needed or ones that would have no place in my new home. I made every effort to *just carry the essentials*. Yet as the years passed, I realized that for every item I eliminated in that move, I somehow ended up with two or more in its place. The issue was not that I failed to rid myself of the unnecessary, but rather it was the lack of shift in my mindset. I made a change in my living space, but did not mentally commit to living without baggage.

When losing weight, if our attitudes and impulses in relation to food and exercise do not change, we quickly regain the weight. If our attitude toward consumerism and the urge to compare and "keep up with the Jones's" does not change, we soon find our homes, cars, and other physical spaces suffocating and cluttered. If our attitudes toward money do not change, we can work for and receive all the promotions and business profits we want, and still live in poverty.

Living lighter is about making a series of ongoing choices — choosing joy over despair, faith over fear, love over indifference, purpose over convenience, intentional nourishment over mindless consumption, and intimate relationship over blind religion.

Reflect:

1. What daily steps do you need to take to live the life you were created for—your best life?

2. What mindsets and attitudes do you need to inculcate to embrace your next season of life?

3. Make a list of what it means to live. What dreams has God given you that you need to begin to work on?

Day 40 – Keep Going. This is Not the End!

"And I am certain that God, who began the good work
within you, will continue his work until it is finally
finished on the day when Christ Jesus returns."
Philippians 1:6 (NLT)

Put your hand over your heart. Is it still beating? Yes?
Then this message is for you. You are here for a reason.
Your life has purpose. Does that goal seem too lofty,
that achievement too distant, those plans impossible,
the call on your life somehow unanswerable? I have 4
words for you:

YOU. CAN. DO. IT.

I was once reminded that sometimes we give up or tap
out, just before we reach the finish line. One night, after
having been notified that school would be closed the
next day due to a coming snowstorm, my 5-year-old son
decided he wanted to watch a movie. Since we knew that
school was already cancelled (thanks to the impending
snow), my husband and I told him that it was fine.
Naturally, however, as a sleepy 5-year-old, attempting
to watch TV past his bedtime, he fell asleep before the
movie reached its end.

The next morning, as he wiped the sleepiness from his
eyes, ready to start the fun of a snow day, he suddenly
remembered that he didn't see 'all' of the movie, and
exclaimed to my husband *"Daddy! The movie didn't finish!"*

Of course, we both chuckled to ourselves. Then my husband responded, with all the seriousness he could muster, "Oh, the movie finished. You just couldn't hang. *You couldn't wait to see the end, and you fell asleep.*"

How many times have we been given a divine assignment, a life-changing opportunity, or a deeply impactful project—with all the ideas and possible positive outcomes—only to get d tired somewhere in the middle. We decide that we can't hang, the process is too long, too hard. We're tired, we don't have time, or we just can't do it.

And then, during our time of prayer, we go to God, like my 5-year-old son, saying *"Hey God! Hey Daddy! What's up?! I thought this was the moment, the opportunity, the project, the assignment that would change my life?! I thought this would turn everything around. I was working hard, but it didn't bear any fruit! It didn't get finished!"*

And He, like my husband, as a loving Father, gently responds, "Hey daughter! There was an expected end, you just couldn't hang. You fell asleep, you slacked off; you gave up."

On this 40th day of your journey, I just want to remind you: "Don't fall asleep before you get to the end." While you may be preparing to close the pages of this book, your pursuit of a life lived lighter is not over. This is a lifelong process, calling us to continually evaluate what we will choose to carry with us along our path in life, eliminate the clutter, and cherish the parts of us that matter most.

There is more in store for you. And if today didn't go as planned, tomorrow is another day to try again. Don't give up.

You can do this!

Reflect:

1. What changes (inward and/or outward) did you see or experience on this journey?

2. List at least two steps you will take to maintain the changes that have taken place.

3. Pray this prayer of thanksgiving with me:

   Lord, I thank you for this 40-day journey you have allowed me to complete. Thank you for the transformation that has started in my heart, the decluttering that has happened in my space, and the lightening of the load I carry in life.

   Whenever I begin to lose sight of my purpose and feel burdened with life experiences, please always remind me to heed Your Word to me when you said: "Come to *me, all you who are weary and burdened, and I will give you rest. Take my yoke upon you and learn from me, for I am gentle and humble in heart, and you will find rest for your souls. For my yoke is easy and my burden is light."*Matthew 11:28-30 (NIV).

Thank you for the grace to go on, and the patience to endure my process. In Jesus' name I pray. Amen

ABOUT THE AUTHOR

*A*ndrea St. Louis is an Educator by calling and profession, and teaching is at the heart of all that she does. She currently serves as a Sunday School and Bible Study teacher at the All Nation Church of God in Springfield, MA. She also works as a Lead Adjunct Professor at a local university, teaching online and on ground, and providing career coaching for non-traditional students.

Andrea is passionate about every opportunity to teach, mentor, and train, and is deeply humbled by the thought that God would use her in the shaping and transforming of minds.

She is a current student in the Master of Arts in Urban Ministry Leadership program at Gordon-Conwell Theological Seminary in Boston, MA. She also holds an MBA in Entrepreneurial Thinking & Innovative Practices from Bay Path University, and a Bachelor's of Science in Management from Saint Joseph College (now the University of Saint Joseph).

Andrea's sincere desire is to help others embrace their purpose, develop language for their calling, and find opportunities to flourish in both their personal and professional lives. She seeks to be a lifelong learner, and encourage others to pursue a greater understanding of the Word of God, the world around them, and the impact they were created to have in this generation for the Kingdom of God.

She is privileged to share her life's journey with her husband, Matthew, and their two beautiful little boys, Ethan and Isaac.

ABOUT HEWLETTE PEARSON

*H*ewlette is a native of Kingston, Jamaica. She migrated to the United States with her parents and brothers, and took up residency in Washington, D.C. As a gifted author, educator, motivator, and pastor, she engages her audiences with humor and empowering messages that foster positive change and move them in the direction of authenticity and success.

In pursuit of excellence in her gifts, Hewlette has earned Master's degrees in Education and Divinity from Johns Hopkins University and Regent University, respectively. She has also earned a diploma from Oxford University, London, England, in religion and politics. Hewlette is an accomplished author of two books, contributing author of two, and have written a few articles in magazines and newsletters, as well. She is also the president of a non-profit organization, iLove Now, that promotes love in communities. The organization's website address is www.ilovenow.org.

She travels within the United States and overseas as keynoter to give empowering speeches, and to deliver messages of hope and love to various audiences. She's been a guest on Radio One stations: 1010FM WOLB and 1340FM WYCB, and NPR Radio 88.9FM WEAA. She conducts a weekly empowerment session, *Monday Morning Empowerment*, on Facebook Live, YouTube, and GospeLive 365FM.

Hewlette's passion in life is encouraging and educating others to be their authentic self and to accomplish extraordinary things that bring joy and fulfillment to their lives. Her life experience and her practice as a speaker, teacher, author, educator, life skills coach, pastor, and friend make her the best at what she does: empower.

For more information about Hewlette, please visit her website at www.HewlettePearson.com. You may contact her by email at Info@HewlettePearson.com.

CONTACT THE AUTHOR

For more information about Andrea St. Louis,
or her speaking engagements and
book signing events, please visit:

www.stepin2purpose.com,

or send an email to

stepin2purpose@gmail.com.

CPSIA information can be obtained
at www.ICGtesting.com
Printed in the USA
FSHW04n1334230418
47281FS